Why

By

Michelle Eades

Dedicated to all the little ones without a voice

Contents

Foreword

It is a sad fact that many people in this country – and all over the world – suffer from abuse at the hands of others. Most suffer in silence, and I was one of them.

This book tells my story, from the horrific events of my childhood to the repercussions they had throughout the rest of my life, looking at their effects both on me and on the rest of my family.

I started writing this book as a way to come to terms with everything that's happened to me, but perhaps – if you're going through a similar thing – it will help you too. Sometimes, knowing that you're not alone can help a great deal, and realising that there are people who care can be the first step to getting on the right path.

I know from experience that it can take you a while to find that correct path, but when you do, it will be more than worth it.

So, here is my story, dedicated to everyone out there who has ever felt the same.

Happy Childhood Summers

"Don't splash, Billy! I'm telling Mum!"

The day was hot, the bright sun beating down on my skinny, swimsuit-clad body. My brother Billy and I were playing in the park, making the most out of the brilliant weather.

It was all going great until I felt a sharp, piercing sensation in my foot, clearly having caught it on something in the pool. I felt tears start to form in my eyes.

"What you crying for, baby?" Billy was staring at me, clearly trying to figure out if I was actually hurt, or if I was just making something out of nothing.

Wincing, I jumped out of the pool and looked at the bottom of my foot. There was blood. Once I'd realised that I was, in fact, bleeding, I started howling like a wounded animal. Billy wasn't much better – he looked down at my foot and immediately went a funny colour. I wondered if my own skin looked that colour, too.

At that moment, the park keeper came over to us, a look of concern on his face. "She alright?"

Billy nodded slowly. "Looks like she's got a bit of glass sticking out of her foot," he said, going an even darker shade of green. Picking me up, he held me against his scrawny chest. "You'll be alright, Mich. I'll get you back home and Mum will sort you out. Don't cry, now."

He struggled with me in his arms, slipping a few times on the wet ground as he carefully made his way towards our house. The park keeper – as well as a few of my friends – followed behind us, like some sort of procession.

It didn't take us long to get back home, which was a basic two-up two-down on a small, narrow street in Deptford. There was an outside toilet and an old tin bath hanging on a nail in the back yard. It wasn't much, but it was home.

By the time our little congregation reached the front door, my ear-splitting howls had decreased to a soft whimper. That is, until my mum answered the door; as soon as I saw her, I started crying again for all I was worth.

Mum stared at me, a look of soft concern on her face. "What's she done?"

"Quick! Take her before I drop her!" By now, Billy was really starting to struggle with the weight of me in his arms, and my mum quickly had me off him.

With no hesitation, she led Billy and the rest of the stragglers into the small living room.

The park keeper stepped forward, seemingly taking charge of the situation. "Looks like she's stepped on a bit of glass. I think it's still in there, too. Caused quite the commotion in the park."

Mum nodded at the park keeper and gently lowered me down onto the floor of the living room. She lifted up my foot so she could have a better look and I immediately felt the pain.

"Don't touch it!" I yelled desperately.

"Shh, there. I just want to have a look."

Knowing that I had to let her look at it, I took a deep breath and covered my eyes with my arms – as if that would make the pain go away. As if it would make everything go away.

"Billy, get me some warm, salted water, will you? I'll also need a clean towel, and the tweezers out of my handbag. OK?"

Billy nodded before running out of the door to do as she'd asked.

When Mum turned her attention back to my foot, I couldn't help but shout out again, "No! Don't touch it, please!" I just couldn't face the pain.

"Come on, Michelle. I've got to get the glass out, or your foot will go all yucky, you understand? Now, you just need to be brave for a little while. It won't take long, and when it's over, I'll give you a penny for some sweets. How does that sound?"

After mulling this over for a second or two, I nodded in agreement. "OK," I simpered, biting on my lip as Billy came back into the room. He'd managed to get everything Mum had asked for.

"Ouch… that hurts… no more, Mum, please!" After a few seconds of protestation from me, the glass was finally out, a plaster was put on my foot, and a penny was put into my hand. My mum smiled at me.

Relieved, I gave her a huge hug and a big, sloppy kiss. "Thanks Mum, I love you."

Her smile widened. "I love you too," she said, giving me a big wet kiss on my cheek.

After my ordeal, I ran off to Aunty Ivy's shop for a penny's worth of sweets, the tears and pain of what had just happened completely forgotten.

If only Mummy's kisses could take all of the tears and the pain away – especially all the pain that 'He' was to cause me later on in my life.

***

I was blessed with a very happy childhood. The youngest of six children, I'm pleased to say that I was spoilt rotten. We only lived in a small house, but it was a house full to the brim of people, of life, and of love. It was also often full of the smell of my Mum's cooking, as well as the sound of laughter coming from all of my siblings. Food and laughter – can there be anything better when you're a child? I was very aware of feeling safe and loved at that time in my life. I couldn't have asked for anything more.

As I've said, I was the youngest of my siblings, and by quite a few years. The eldest, Sharon, was twenty-one years older than me. Then there were twenty years between me and Al, sixteen years between me and Lydia, fourteen years between me and Pam, and then there was Billy, who was just six years my senior.

Apart from Billy, I don't have many childhood memories of my other siblings, apart from when my eldest brother, Al, got married. For this special occasion, I have vague recollections of being a bridesmaid along with my niece, Jane. We were both decked out in the same frock, we had halos made of pretty flowers, and we wore shiny satin shoes on our feet. The memory of this outfit has always stood out vividly for me.

Jane was only fourteen months younger than me, so we inevitably spent a lot of time together, either playing in the local park or in the adventure playground by my sister Lydia's house. We did it all: swinging on ropes held on by tiny threads, climbing up wooden structures that creaked and swung under our weight, and pushing one another as high as we could on the old tyre swings. Nowadays, these kinds of activities would probably be abolished under the 'health and safety' act, but it never did us any harm. We were always out and about, playing in the sun – we hated staying inside, where it was dull and boring. We liked to feel the wind on our faces as we raced to the park, liked to look up and see the sun shining through the leaves of the trees, making shapes on our skin. You didn't get that if you stayed inside. We filled our days with run-outs with my younger nieces and nephew, not going back in until either our bellies started rumbling or we were called in for dinner.

I remember those days so well.

These memories are the things I try to hold onto from my childhood, desperately clinging onto my innocence until 'He' took it all away, ruining my 'Happy Days' and my memories of them forever. He crept into my life, casting a shadow over everything that was good, pushing it all away from me, forever.

***

My Mum was always my hero. She could make anything right, no matter how bad things felt at the time; all she needed to do was wrap me up in her big, squishy arms, and I would feel content – like nothing and no one could get to me or bring me down.

She was my idol.

Now, don't get me wrong, I loved my dad dearly, but he was the strict one of the two – not really a cuddly dad, exactly – and therefore seemed in direct contrast with my mum. He was always there, though, for which I was grateful.

Still, the house always felt different when Mum wasn't around – colder, and empty.

Both of my parents worked, Dad as a painter and decorator and Mum as a worker in a tin making factory. It was always Mum's arms which I ran to when she came home from work, or when she picked me up from school, always her I would run to with the painting I'd done for her during class, or when I had hurt myself or was unwell. Just the smell of her, the feel of her, the very presence of her, would make me feel safe. Being wrapped in her arms was like being wrapped in a magic blanket, where no bad thing in the world could get to me or hurt me.

I know a lot of people probably have these memories of their parents from when they were little, but they are so vivid to me, even now. All I have to do is picture myself being in her arms and I can remember the exact feeling of safety that I felt back then. The exact same feeling of being loved unconditionally.

Of course, I have other memories of her from when I was a child, like her cleaning the doorstep with her hair in curlers and a scarf around her head. Or her beating the rugs in the yard, or the click click click of her knitting needles as she sat working on the sofa, luring me into a deep, cotton candy-filled sleep as I sat beside her.

These are the things a child should remember, and I *do* remember them, dearly, but these days, those wonderful memories get pushed aside to let the darker ones in, memories that no child should have to keep locked up tight in the back of their mind.

These memories come creeping in, laughing at me, ridiculing me, reaching out to me in places where Mum can't find me, where she can't wrap me in her arms. They taunt me as I scream for her, desperately shouting for her in the middle of my dark, hellish nightmares, but she doesn't come.

Why doesn't she come?

The Big Mansion

I felt like a princess.

"It's a big mansion!" I said to my niece, brimming with excitement. We were moving house today, and compared to the two-up two-down we'd all been squeezed into for years, a mansion is exactly what our new home looked like, especially to my small eyes. It was going to be brilliant.

Turning to my niece, Jane, I couldn't help but smile. "Follow me!" I shouted, leading her to the top of the four storey house we were moving into – four whole storeys! I couldn't believe it.

The adults were busy getting the furniture in, and I vaguely wondered how we would ever have enough beds and sofas and tables and chairs to fill this huge space.

Jane was looking around at her surroundings in awe. "Wow, it's huge. I wish I could live here!"

I beamed at my niece. "Well, you can stay over whenever you want. You can all stay – it's big enough!" With that, we ran in and out of all the rooms and up and down all the stairs, completely amazed by how much room we had to play in.

Of course, I had to share my room with my sister, Sharon, and her daughter, Marie, but I didn't mind at all; I loved Marie as if she were my very own sister. She was only a little over a year old, but as she grew, so did our bond.

It was also great having my big sister, Sharon, around as well; I was only really just getting to know her. This was in part because she'd been in the Air Force for almost four years, and partly because – being only six years old when we moved – she had seemed like a stranger to me when she'd returned home.

The most exciting thing for me about the new house was having a bathroom and toilet that was actually inside – no more going out into the cold for me!

Those days were great. We all settled into our new home in New Cross and the whole summer was filled with sleepovers with my nieces, and playing all around the house as well as outside. You see, on top of having a nice big house, we also had the luxury of having our own back garden to play in. It wasn't just a yard with a few paving slabs in, either, but a proper garden with proper grass. I couldn't believe my luck.

I remember those days as being some of the happiest of my life, but this was all about to change.

***

"Where are we going, Dad?"

Little did I know how the answer to those five words would change my life forever.

"We're going to see Aunty Betty and Uncle Charlie," he replied.

I didn't remember meeting this Aunty Betty or Uncle Charlie before; I didn't even remember hearing them mentioned before. "Do they have children for me to play with, Dad?"

"No children," I remember him saying.

I was a bit disappointed with his reply, but I didn't mind too much; it was still an adventure to me.

I can't recall every detail of this visit, but I do remember seeing an old lady in a hospital bed in one room, as well as sitting in the kitchen with a little man who had round glasses on his face and braces on his trousers. This was Uncle Charlie, and he seemed nice.

When Mum and Dad went in to see Aunty Betty in the hospital bed, Uncle Charlie gave me some biscuits and milk. That's all I remember.

The visit was soon over and then we were setting off home in the car.

I don't recall ever seeing Aunty Betty again, but I do recall seeing Uncle Charlie. I *definitely* recall this, and I wished now that I didn't, that all memories of him were completely erased from my mind.

If only.

***

I don't know how much time had passed when I next saw Uncle Charlie – it could have been weeks or it could have been months – but one day, he came round our house for dinner.

I remember wondering who was looking after Aunty Betty, and when I asked him, he responded with, "She's in Heaven."

He was still nice to me after this, but I do remember feeling mildly uncomfortable around him, because he wanted me to sit on his lap a lot. Unfortunately, as I was still so young, my senses weren't finely tuned enough and I didn't know how to convert that uncomfortable feeling into the warning that it was meant to be.

His visits to our house became more and more frequent, and it got to the point that he'd come round at least a couple of times a week. He always brought sweets for me and always wanted to talk to me about school and what I'd done that day. It all seemed pretty innocent, but that's when there were other people around.

Then, one day, I was left in the house alone with him.

Mum had turned to me and said, "Get your coat on, Michelle, we're going down the shop."

I really wasn't in the mood, and when I asked her if I had to go, she responded that I couldn't stay in the house on my own.

This is when Uncle Charlie piped up. "I'll watch her," he said, smiling. "She can stay here with me."

Mum considered this for a few moments, and then agreed. She told us that she wouldn't be more than twenty minutes, and then she was gone.

Once she'd left, Uncle Charlie went to the toilet, and I vaguely remember hearing the front room door open as he came back. I was busy standing in the middle of the living room, watching the TV.

Then, I felt him as he came up right behind me.

"Do you like cartoons?" he asked me. It was a perfectly innocent question, made not innocent at all by the fact that he then pushed himself into my back and started to rub my shoulders.

When I felt something hard pushing into me, I stepped away, and just at that moment, my mum returned.

Not saying a word, he went into the kitchen with her, as if nothing had happened.

I remember feeling confused. I knew that something weird had just occurred, but I wasn't sure *what*, exactly. Alarm bells would have been ringing if I'd been older, I'm sure, but right then, he was just my Uncle Charlie.

When he came back into the living room with my mum, he said goodbye, kissed me on the cheek, and left.

I sat down to watch the TV and the strange occurrence with Uncle Charlie completely left my mind. It didn't seem important; after all, he was only asking me if I liked cartoons, wasn't he?

***

Maybe a week or so passed before I saw him again.

By that time, what had happened in the living room had completely faded from my mind, but when he came into the house again, I immediately felt uneasy. It was difficult to explain, but perhaps those alarm bells *were* actually going off back then – I was just too young to understand what they meant.

It was either during this visit or his next, I'm not sure, but I was in my back garden when he came out to talk to me. I remember I was playing on the slide.

"You know, Michelle," he said, slowly, as if trying to figure out what to say next. "Sometimes, children have to keep grown-up secrets." He looked around to check no one was around to overhear him. "And when children *don't* keep adults' secrets, then those children get taken away from their mums and dads. They never see them again, do you understand?" I didn't say anything, and he continued. "I've known other little girls who told about my adult secret and they were taken away. Now, *you* wouldn't ever tell a secret and get taken away from your mum, would you?"

I shook my head in response, not quite understanding all that he was saying, but knowing above all else that I would never want to be taken away from my mum. That was a no-brainer.

After the encounter in the garden, I'm not sure how long it was before I saw him again – times and dates have got lost somewhere in my memory along the way, as often happens – but the memory of what happened when we next met will stay in my mind forever.

Innocence Gone

One day, I was upstairs at home when the sound of voices coming from my kitchen made me go down to investigate. Even before I saw him, I knew that the voice belonged to Uncle Charlie, and it stopped me in my tracks. Again, that uneasy feeling washed over me, and although I didn't understand why, I was hesitant as I entered the kitchen.

"Hello Michelle," he said, giving me a wink, which my mum didn't see as she was busy making the tea.

Without responding, I went and sat down at the table.

My mum turned to me then, smiling. "We've got to pop out to the shop in a while," she said.

Before I even got the chance to reply, Charlie responded for me. "That's OK. You can leave her here with me; she'll be fine."

I looked straight into his eyes. "It's alright, I want to go with Mum."

This time, my mum responded for him. "No, it's alright. Wait here with Uncle Charlie; I won't be long." With that decided, she put on her coat, picked up her purse, and walked out the door.

With Mum gone, the room was deadly quiet, and Uncle Charlie made me jump when he said, "Why don't you go upstairs and watch TV? I'll be up when I've finished my tea."

Without waiting another second, I ran upstairs, feeling scared but not really knowing why, and within just a few minutes he was in the living room with me.

"What are you watching?" he asked. "Why don't you turn it over? See if there's anything else on?"

I got up off the sofa to turn the TV channel over, and as soon as I did, he was behind me. He started to massage my shoulders and I completely tensed up.

"Remember what I said about secrets?" he said, and before I knew what was happening, I heard the sound of him unzipping his trousers. Then, he grabbed my hand and put it on the hard part of his body, making me rub it up and down.

The whole time this was happening, I was just standing there, completely frozen. I wanted to run, but it was as if I was glued to the floor. I definitely knew this was wrong, but there simply wasn't anything I could do about it.

After Charlie had finished what he was doing, he bent down and whispered in my ear. "This is our little secret, and if you tell anyone, they won't believe you. You're just a little girl, so no one will believe you. If you do say anything, they'll take you away from your mum and dad for lying."

With that said, he sat down on the sofa and started to watch the TV, casually chatting to me as if nothing had happened.

I just sat on the arm chair, my eyes fixed to the television, trying to make sense in my young mind of what exactly had just happened. I knew deep down that what he'd done was wrong, but worse was the fear that I'd be taken away from my parents. I just couldn't let that happen.

Not long after, my mum came back, and the first thing she asked was, "You been a good girl?"

Uncle Charlie looked straight at me and said, "She's as good as gold, ain't ya?"

I nodded and mumbled something about playing upstairs, running up to my bedroom before anyone else could say anything.

I remember just sitting on my bed and feeling numb. I was very scared, and there were a lot of mixed thoughts going round and round in my head. I just couldn't understand what had happened, or why Uncle Charlie would do something like that.

I wanted to tell Mum, tell her to never let him in again – I really did – but if I did that, if I told her our secret, I was absolutely positive that I would never see her again.

I stayed there in my bedroom, thinking and worrying, until Mum shouted up to come and say goodbye to Uncle Charlie.

Slowly, I walked to the top of the stairs. "Bye Uncle Charlie," I said, in no more than a whisper, unable to raise my voice.

He replied to me, "Bye, see you next time!"

I physically felt myself shake. Next time… next time… those words just kept going round and round in my head.

I didn't want there to be a next time.

***

From that day on, whenever he would come over, he'd say to my mum, "If you need to pop out, don't worry about dragging Michelle along with you. She can stay here with me; we always find ways of having fun, don't we?" He'd say this while looking directly at me, something which chilled me to the core.

Sometimes, Mum didn't need to go out, and I was so thankful whenever this happened. But, of course, sometimes she *did* need to go out, and at these times, I would scream inside my head, 'Don't go, Mum! Please don't go!'

It was as if Charlie *knew*: he knew exactly how long Mum would be gone, he knew exactly what he was going to do, and he knew exactly how long it would take. Sometimes he would make me rub him – like the first time – but on the occasions when Mum had gone shopping further afield, the abuse would be much, much worse.

I remember the first time that he forced that hard thing in my mouth. He pushed my head back and forth until I tasted the salty, sickly taste of him, and the first few times it happened, I physically threw up; it was that bad.

This was when he would get angry with me, shouting at me and asking me if I was trying to let people in on our secret. He would say, "You know what's gonna happen to you if you do, don't you?" I nodded my head, silently, praying that I wouldn't throw up again. "Then stop being sick!"

I would try and keep the gagging down, try and keep the sick from coming up my throat, but it was difficult.

***

I don't remember much about starting at Junior School.

What should have been a happy, exciting time was actually the opposite. I felt like an empty shell, holding this secret inside me when I so desperately wanted to be able to tell someone. Holding onto this knowledge would either make me really quiet and withdrawn, or really hyper and smiley – this was because I was worried that someone would ask me what was wrong, and then I would be taken away from my mum, like Charlie had told me so many times before.

Due to school, his visits were less frequent now, but sometimes on a Sunday, while Mum was cooking and while Dad was down the pub, he would find a way to either touch me or make me touch him.

I vividly recall one Sunday. Mum was in the bathroom, and everyone else was out – I don't recall where – leaving just me and him alone.

He pushed me up against the living room door, unzipped his trousers, and then stuck his hand under my dress and down my knickers. He then forced his fingers inside, and tears filled my eyes with the pain of it, but he didn't care. He just put his mouth over mine and started rubbing himself with his other hand.

When it was over, he said, "You better go play in your room; I don't want anyone to see that you've been crying. You know what will happen if you tell!"

I ran to my bedroom then, diving under the covers and weeping until I felt that I'd cried everything out. My private parts were throbbing from where he had hurt me.

I felt so alone. I felt like *I* was bad – that it was somehow *my* fault because I'd 'let him' do it to me. It didn't even occur to me that even if I'd tried, I wouldn't have been able to stop him doing it. Plus, I was too scared of what the consequences would be if I told everyone.

He was counting on that, and it worked. It worked for far too long.

When I went to get in the bath that evening, I took off my underwear and noticed some red stuff in them. This shocked me badly; I thought that, because I was bleeding, I was going to die, but even then I said nothing. Instead, I threw the knickers in the bin where Mum wouldn't find them, had my bath, and went to bed.

Of course, I couldn't sleep. I just lay awake, staring at the ceiling, having thoughts of running away and never coming back. But I knew that would never happen; I was too scared. Too scared to go, and too scared to tell anyone. I was just going to have to put up with it and hope that it stopped soon. I would just carry on keeping quiet, like I'd been doing the whole time.

I felt like I had no other choice.

***

The abuse carried on and on, for what seemed like an eternity. No matter what was going on or who was around, he would always find a way or a place, and I would always keep our secret, fearing that I would be ripped away from my family, never to see any of them again. I just wished that he'd stop.

I wished that he'd go away and never come back.

Then, one Sunday morning, I got my wish.

I heard my dad's voice coming from the kitchen, talking about a man. "I don't know how he died… heart attack, I think."

I walked slowly into the kitchen, looking up at him and asking, "Who died, Dad?"

Both of my parents looked at me then, as if unsure how to tell me.

Eventually, my Mum replied. "Uncle Charlie died. I'm sorry, I know you liked him, but he's in Heaven now."

I didn't say anything in response to this. Instead, I just turned and walked out of the kitchen.

Looking back, my mum and dad must have thought that I hadn't said anything because I was so upset, but of course, that wasn't it.

Uncle Charlie was gone. I felt like a bird that had been set free from its cage! I ran upstairs without a care in the world and sat down to watch TV, feeling the happiest I could remember feeling in such a long, long time.

I had such a huge smile on my face, and even though I wanted to jump up and down and laugh with relief, I didn't. I didn't want my parents asking any awkward questions.

I just remember thinking: 'I bet he's not really in Heaven!' But wherever he was, I would never have to see him or think about him ever again.

***

If only this were true.

Although he was gone, I wasn't free; the aftermath of what he had done to me was going to follow me throughout my life, coming to the forefront a few years later with some devastating effects.

I Don't Care

For the rest of my junior years, I felt relatively unscathed by what had happened – I'd had a lucky escape, he was dead now, and I was grateful that he was gone.

But, of course, this didn't stop him from appearing in my nightmares.

I couldn't protect myself from him when I was asleep.

Then, everything changed. When I was around twelve years old, we moved onto the Ferrier Estate in SE3. I didn't really go out much during this time – I just kept myself to myself, as I didn't really feel like I belonged anywhere. I just felt different to other kids my age. I couldn't really explain it.

Then, one day, something in my life shifted.

It came out of nowhere. It's an extremely hard thing to try and describe, but I just woke up one morning and felt like a totally different person; it was as if I'd gone to bed as my usual self, and then had woken up as someone else – someone completely new.

The main emotion I felt at that time was anger, and it was so incredibly intense. Looking back, I think this was the beginning of the depression and despair that continued through my teens and followed me right into my adulthood.

Basically, I wanted to fuck the world off – to follow my own rules and nobody else's. This included my family, and I started ignoring anything that my mum or dad had to say to me. I just didn't want to know. I started truanting from school, hanging around the estate with another group of 'I don't give a fuck' teenagers and just wasting our days away. By that point, I was well on my way to self-destruction.

It was around this time that I had my first sexual experience with another woman. Thinking back, I'd always felt 'different' compared to most of my friends. For instance, I remember playing kiss chase at infant school, but I'd always wanted to be on the boy's side, chasing the girls instead. So it was always there, I just didn't realise what it meant. As I grew, so did my attraction to the same sex.

So, my first time. Her name was Katie, and she was about ten months younger than me. She went to the same school I did and she'd started to come round my house to have somewhere to go when we couldn't be bothered to go to school and 'hopped the wag' instead. She was very popular with the boys, but I had a feeling that there might be something special between us.

I was right.

One night, she stayed over, and we got onto the topic of sexual preferences. "Have you always known you fancy girls, then?" asked Kate, straight and to the point.

"Yeah, I've never fancied boys," I replied, wondering where this was going.

"What's it like? To do it with a girl, I mean?"

I laughed. "Well, obviously I enjoy it! But it's hard to say what it's like." I shrugged. I didn't know what else to say.

After that conversation, we listened to music for a while and then I turned off the light and got into my bed. I remember having this feeling – that something was going to happen. Something between me and Kate.

I wanted it to happen – I really did – but I was just too nervous to lead the way myself.

I didn't have to worry, however, as after just a few minutes, I felt her stroking my hair. Holding my breath, I could feel my heart pumping away in my chest as I waited for something else to happen.

Quietly, she whispered, "You awake?"

I hesitated, but only for a second. "Yes."

"Then turn over."

I turned to face her, not knowing what I was going to do, and before I knew it, she'd put her tongue in my mouth and had started to kiss me. That kiss was something I remember vividly; it was the start of something new and exciting.

That whole night was glorious – a night I would never forget – for not only was she the first girl who I made love to, but it also confirmed what I already knew: that I was definitely a lesbian, and that I was never going to sleep with a man.

I guess that most people fall hard for their first love, and this was certainly true for me – I fell head over heels for Kate. We met up as much as we could, and those meetings would almost always end up with us making love.

I say almost…

I have one memory that seems funny now, but it certainly didn't seem that way at the time.

One day, my sister Sharon was over visiting Mum. She had two children by that time – her daughter, Marie, and her son, James. For some reason, my nephew James loved following me around – I mean, he followed me *everywhere* – and on this particular day I was taking the train to go and see Kate.

As ever, he was eager to tag along. "Can I come?" he asked.

"No," I said, "not today."

Anyway, I got on the train (from Kidbrooke to Blackheath) and had just gone through the ticket barrier when I heard a small voice behind me say, "My aunt's paying for my ticket."

Turning round, I saw James talking to the ticket inspector. I was furious that he'd followed me, but I couldn't exactly leave him there to get into trouble for fare evasion, so I reluctantly bought him a ticket and took him with me.

So, I arrived at Kate's house with my little nephew in tow, and Kate and I spent the whole afternoon watching TV with my chaperone. Neither of us were too impressed with the way the day had played out.

Thinking back, this is a bittersweet memory for me; these days, I'd give anything for James to be that annoying little nephew again, following me around everywhere like I was his favourite person in the whole world.

So, even though it was annoying at the time, I remember that day with a smile on my face.

***

By now, I had been seeing Kate for about six months. I was still coming home late, skipping school, drinking with friends, and generally just acting out. Mum, Dad, and the rest of my family couldn't understand why I was behaving this way; they just put it down to me being a 'naughty teenager', rebelling against the system and authority figures, as many other people my age did.

The more they asked me why I was doing these things, the more I pulled away. I didn't have to explain myself or how I was feeling to them; I couldn't.

Of course, just when I thought there wasn't any more trouble I could get myself into, I found some. This came in the form of a couple of guys who lived on the Ferrier Estate and who were wanted by the police for armed robbery. I – along with Kate and a few other friends – started hanging out with them. All the teenagers I knew started going to their flat to get drunk, smoke dope, and have sex, and if you weren't involved in this scene, then you were considered a nobody. I certainly didn't want to be a nobody.

This meant that we had somewhere else to go when we were truanting from school, somewhere where there weren't any adults, and there definitely weren't any rules. Although I never touched drugs, I did indulge in alcohol, getting pissed every day and spending most of my evenings with my head down the toilet. I would either go home in the early hours of the morning, or not at all. It became my new routine.

While all this was going on, I started to notice that Kate was changing. She seemed different, somehow… distant. She'd started spending a lot more time with one of the guys who owned the flat, and it wasn't long before she started sleeping with him. I was devastated – I hadn't seen it coming, not at all, and I didn't know how to handle it.

That was the first time I cut.

Completely drunk, I swayed out of the flat, with a razor blade I'd taken from the bathroom, and found a quiet place on the green. Lying down on the cold grass, I stared up at the sky as tears fell down my face. I couldn't stop them. I didn't want to stop them. I felt so alone out there.

I started telling myself that there was something wrong with me – why else would Kate do that to me? Nothing was going right. Nothing at all.

I felt an aching coming from deep inside me, as if I was trying to reach for something that just wasn't there.

I took the razor blade from my pocket.

I could see *his* face in front of me – mocking me – and I couldn't help but feel all of the pain he'd put me through seeping through my entire body. It was as if it was happening right there and then. As if Uncle Charlie had never died, and would never die – at least, not for me.

I don't remember the first cut, I just remember watching in fascination as the warm blood trickled down my arm. With each cut, I felt a little better – it was as if the lid had been taken off a steam cooker, the release magical and calming.

After a while my tears stopped, and I just sat there on the grass, alone, letting myself feel the pain. I don't know how long I sat there for, but eventually I got up and found my way home.

By the time I'd gone into the bathroom to assess the damage, the blood had started to congeal on my arm and it was stinging like hell. I cleaned it up as best I could, and headed downstairs to my parents, hoping they wouldn't think I was mad.

My dad was asleep in the armchair, but my mum was still up knitting. "What time do you call this?" she asked, as it was about 2 a.m.

"Don't start, Mum," I replied. "I've just been round a mate's." I paused, not really knowing what to say or how to say it. In the end I just said, "Have we got any bandages? I twisted my ankle and it hurts like mad." I was hoping she wouldn't see through the lie, and if she did, she didn't let on.

Instead, she just got up and rummaged around in a drawer in the kitchen. "Do you want me to put it on?" she asked, holding up a crêpe bandage in her hand.

"No, it's alright, I can do it," I insisted, before adding, "thanks, Mum." Kissing her, I went up to my room.

After I dressed my arm with the bandage, I lay down on my bed, fully clothed. Everything was just zooming around in my mind.

What I had done had frightened me, and I felt guilty for treating Mum the way I did. Even with that, I still felt angry – incredibly angry – because of what had happened with Uncle Charlie, and the fact that she hadn't stopped him.

Oh, I know, she didn't know what was going on, but I was still angry with her. After all, she was my *mum* – shouldn't she have known that something had been going on? Shouldn't she have just been able to look at me and *know*, on some deep, intuitive level, that something was wrong? It made no sense, of course, but I wasn't exactly thinking clearly.

As I went to sleep, there was a whole load of emotions going through my mind. The last thing I thought of, before I drifted off into an uneasy slumber, was that I was going to have to start wearing long sleeves.

Nightmares

I'm in a lift, and I'm going up. I know that the top floor is a no-go area – completely off limits – and so I reach out to press the big, round button with a number one on: the first floor. The lift, however, goes past it, continuing on and on until, finally, it opens on the top floor. I step out into a dark corridor, quickly regretting it and turning back to press for the lift – but the lift door is gone. I'm trapped. I suddenly realise how cold I am, and as I exhale, my breath lets out a steam of white air. Suddenly, I can hear footsteps coming along the corridor, getting faster and faster as the person starts running towards me. Even without seeing, I know that it's *him*; I can smell his breath as he gets nearer, and then he reaches out his hands to rip at my clothes. I'm screaming and screaming and he's laughing and laughing, and then I wake up, damp with sweat, knowing that even from the cold depths of Hell, he still wants me.

This dream – this nightmare – has been a recurring one over the years, and I still have it even to this day.

Back then, after the cutting incident, I was having trouble sleeping. As soon as my eyes closed and sleep engulfed me, I would be taken back to that place of pain and uncertainty.

I drank tea and coffee, watched movies, did pretty much anything I could to keep me awake, but no matter what I did, the nightmares just kept on coming.

During the day, I would meet up with the crowd of boys at the flat and drink whatever alcoholic beverages were lying around. I wanted to take myself back to a happier time and place, but all that happened was that I'd vomit myself back to reality, where the same pain, guilt, and anger was still alive within me.

The guys at the flat I went to would always make out with the teenage girls that hung out there, but for some reason they left me alone. It was as if they knew it wouldn't be in their interest to approach me, which I – of course – didn't much care about anyway.

The days and nights rolled into weeks, and my visits home became less and less frequent.

I was losing myself, but I didn't notice.

***

I don't know who exactly told my dad and my brother Billy where I was, but I woke up one morning in the flat to a loud hammering on the door.

They were standing there on the doorstep, along with some other parents whose teenagers often used the flat as their place of retreat.

Without wasting a second, my dad said, "Come on you."

I followed him home without any argument, and once we'd got inside, he turned to me and explained. "The police are going up there. I don't ever want to find you there again."

That was it. That was *all* that was said on the matter.

In my head, I was screaming, 'Don't you want to know *why*? Don't you care? Is that all you have to say?'

My mum wasn't much better; when she saw me she just gave me a hug and then carried on with what she was doing. There was no demanding an explanation, no shouting at me, nothing.

After that, I went to my bedroom and just lay there for a long time, thinking. My parents were prepared to simply put all of my behaviour down to being 'out of control', 'a bad girl with no respect', just 'going through normal teenage stuff'. Not one single person had asked the most simple of questions: why?

Of course, in all honesty, I don't know what I would have said if they *had* asked me. I doubt whether I would have tried to explain; after all, I was drowning in my own anger and I wanted those around me to suffer too.

The next thing I heard, the guys from the flat had gone on the run and the police were looking for them.

So that put a stop to everyone's favourite hangout.

***

It was nearing my 16th birthday, and by then I'd met another girl, Marion. We started having a relationship and I began to think that things were looking up. I mean, I was still having nightmares and I barely ever got any sleep, but I had a focus now: someone who needed me, and I them.

I was excited about my upcoming birthday, and I asked my mum if I could have a party.

"Oh, I don't know about that," was her reply. "I'm not sure your dad will let you."

I wasn't going to back down that easily, and I pleaded with her to make it happen. "Oh, go on, Mum. I've never had a birthday party before, and after all, I'm going to be *sixteen*."

Eventually, she said that she'd think about it, and that she'd also speak to Dad. I knew that meant yes.

Once I'd got the go ahead, I invited everyone I wanted to the party, and when the evening came, it got off to a good start. There was music and laughter and I felt better than I had done in a very long time.

The party had been in full swing for a couple of hours when the trouble started.

Gatecrashers had tried to get into the house pretty early on, but they'd been sent on their way with a flea in their ear. Living on an estate like the Ferrier, however, I knew that this wouldn't be the end of it.

Sure enough, within half an hour a crowd had gathered outside, and a fight erupted between the genuine party guests and those trying to crash it. It was chaos: bottles were being thrown, hair was being pulled, and there were bundles of people hanging around on the green outside my house.

It wasn't long before someone called the police, and once the sirens were heard in the distance, everyone took off. When the police got there, they took a statement off us and then left.

All was quiet by now, and I went up to my room to be alone. I was bruised but satisfied that it was now all over.

I was wrong.

The next morning, I woke up and went downstairs to see both of my parents sitting in the living room. Neither of them looked good, and it was clear that they hadn't slept.

I asked what happened, and that's when I found out everything. After I'd gone to my room, the crowd had come back, looking for another fight. This time, my dad was hit by a bottle, and my mum was thrown to the floor, where she proceeded to get her hands stamped on by the gatecrashers. My brothers and sisters had been there and had been trying to pull the people off my parents when, again, the sirens of the police drove the crowd away.

Mum and Dad had been taken to the hospital, and once they'd been looked over, they were discharged in the early hours. Both of them were bruised but they didn't have any serious injuries, thank God.

I was mortified. I couldn't believe that I'd slept through the whole thing. I felt so guilty – after all, none of this would have happened if I hadn't insisted on having a party in the first place.

Bad things followed me around. Nothing good ever seemed to happen to me.

Again, the feeling of needing a release overwhelmed me, and I sat in the bath cutting into my skin. I deserved the pain I was inflicting on myself.

That night, I had another nightmare. *He* had me, and as he was pulling me down, I screamed out, "Mum!" I woke then, my heart pounding, and I remember thinking, 'She never came'.

Still trying to get my breath back, I lay down and waited for the sun to rise.

***

Soon after this incident we moved off the estate, meaning that my relationship with Marion had to come to an end.

Another chapter of my life, however, was about to begin.

Better The Devil You Know

We hadn't long moved to Ladywell when Dad had a stroke. He was walking along the street when it happened, and after he'd fallen over, people just stepped over him – they thought he was drunk. Luckily, the police had found him and realised that it wasn't drink related at all. Thank God.

The stroke had caused a bleed on his brain, and he needed surgery. After this, he initially seemed to recover quite well, but within a few months he'd started to get confused and slur his words a little. It was heart-breaking to see.

I tried to help out as much as I could. While Mum was at work, I would make sure that Dad had something to eat, and I also made sure that he kept up with everyday tasks, such as shaving. For the first time in my life, I found myself using a razor to shave a man, rather than using it on myself to self-harm.

Unfortunately, it wasn't long before my dad's condition worsened and he passed away at Lewisham hospital.

I was devastated, and not just because he'd died – the loss of my dad made me realise just how distant I had become from my parents. Having to witness the pain of my mum's loss was awful, and I decided there and then that the blame I'd put on them – and her, in particular – for what had happened to me all those years ago was not justified at all. From that moment on, we became a lot closer.

It was around this time that I met the third woman I was to become involved with, and although I had no idea back then, this was a relationship that would last for thirteen years.

Her name was Micky, and I met her through my friend, Mag.

One day, Mag turned to me and said, completely out of the blue, "There's a nice girl who lives just across the road. She's single… I think you'd make a great couple."

Before I could utter any kind of response, Mag left, coming back a few minutes later with an Asian person whom she introduced to me as 'Micky'. At the time I remember thinking that this couldn't possibly be the 'girl' she was talking about – Micky was surely a boy!

Anyway, I said hi to Micky and Micky said hello back. She continued, "My name is Fatima but everyone calls me Micky."

Her voice was pretty feminine, and that's when I realised that she was, indeed, a 'she'.

"You'll have to excuse the state of me," she carried on. "I've been decorating my mum's house ready for my sister's wedding."

I didn't know what to say. I didn't care what she looked like or why – she was way too masculine for me. I wasn't interested. Not one bit.

After some small talk, I got out of there, telling myself 'no way' as I closed the door.

Well, as the saying goes, 'you can't help who you fall in love with', something which I definitely started to relate to.

Micky and I met up a few more times at my friend's house, and then we became an item. The relationship became quite serious quite quickly, and although her mum didn't like me, we decided to move into a flat together.

The day we moved was not a good day.

I knew that Micky's mum didn't like the idea of us moving in together, but I never thought she'd do something as drastic as calling the police – which, of course, she did.

When the police arrived, Micky's mum was holding me against the wall by my top. Looking perplexed, one of the officers asked what was going on, to which her mum replied, "She's stealing my Fatima!"

Still obviously confused, the police officer looked at me and told me, "Give the lady back her Fatima."

I couldn't help but giggle as I pointed to Micky. "That is Fatima."

The poor officer looked even more bewildered as he turned to Micky's mum and asked her to explain.

"She's taking Fatima away to live with her," she replied.

On hearing this, the officer asked how old I was (eighteen) and how old Micky was (seventeen). Then, they stood by as we packed the rest of her things, making sure there was no more trouble from Micky's mum.

After that, although she put up with me for Micky's sake, we knew where the battle lines had been drawn. We were both on the same page.

***

We soon settled into our flat, and while Micky worked at the family shop, I started working as a carer in a residential home for the elderly.

At first, things were good between us. We were happy. I even left work to help out in Micky's family business, but after a few years, things started to sour.

Micky would take off for days at a time, leaving me behind, not knowing where she'd gone or what she was doing, and desperately worried for her safety.

Then, on her return from one of these disappearing acts – for which she would give me no explanation whatsoever – we were invited to a night out with a couple of friends who we'd met at a gay bar in Lewisham. After the bar closed, we all decided to go back to one of the friends' flats for a drink.

By this point, I was the worse for wear – after having had rather a lot of alcohol – and I'd been sitting in the living room with Fran for a while when I noticed that Micky and Liz were missing.

I kept trying to get up to go and look for them, but Fran kept pulling me back into the living room to 'talk'. Eventually, the night caught up with me, and I fell asleep on the sofa.

The next morning when I woke up, Micky was sleeping next to me.

That day, I kept on thinking about the night before. What had happened was rather hazy, of course, but as the day went on, snippets of the evening kept returning to me – for instance, Micky's disappearance at Liz's flat.

I had a horrible feeling in the pit of my stomach, a sickly feeling that wouldn't go away. And I knew it wasn't the alcohol.

The following morning, I couldn't ignore the feeling – that Liz and Micky had been together – any longer. Psyching myself up, I went to Liz's flat and knocked on the door. While I was waiting for her to appear, I tried to think of what I would say, but I had no idea. As it turned out, when Liz opened the door, I just came out with, "Micky told me what happened the other night."

She immediately went bright red, and I knew there and then that I was right.

Anyway, she invited me in and then led me into her kitchen, where she stood nervously by the counter. "It was a mistake," she said. "The drink and that…"

I couldn't believe what I was hearing. "So having sex with my girlfriend was just a mistake?" Bile was rising in my throat.

Liz looked down at the floor. "I'm sorry."

By this point, I could barely look at her, I was so angry. "*Sorry*? Let me tell you this – if you so much as *look* in Micky's direction again, you'll regret it!" With that, I called her a few choice names and then left, slamming the door behind me.

Once I was outside, that familiar feeling started to travel through me – one of sickness, fear, and excitement. The only way I knew how to cope with these emotions was to cut, and a little while later, I had blood oozing out of my arm and I felt much better.

I felt ready to confront Micky with what I knew.

When she came home, I started the evening as usual, with a bit of small talk about her day. I felt calm.

Then, after about an hour of sitting in front of the TV with Micky, I said simply, "I know."

She turned to look at me, frowning. "Know what?"

I took a deep breath. "Everything."

When she tried to deny any knowledge, I carried on. "Don't take me for a fool, Micky. Liz told me everything – you know, about having sex upstairs in her bedroom? While I was in the living room below you?"

Of course, she denied it at first, that is, until I offered to take her round Liz's flat so we could confront her together. *Then* the tears started.

"I'm sorry," she said. "Please don't leave me! I don't know why I did it… she just came onto me. I promise you, it will never happen again." She was grovelling, desperate. I wasn't sure how to take it.

As I sat there listening, I thought to myself that I had to forgive her. I didn't want to be on my own – I *couldn't* be on my own. So, although deep down I didn't believe her promises for a single second, I agreed to put it behind us and start afresh.

The thought of leaving her, and having to start all over again with someone new, scared the hell out of me.

This relationship was familiar, and that, I felt, was enough.

Sex Change

Well, Micky's infidelities continued, and so did my forgiveness. I just didn't want to be on my own, and I dealt with it the only way I knew how – with the help of a razor blade. It was the only way I could release the pain, get it out of my body, out of my mind…

We carried on as if everything was fine; we even went on a six week long holiday to Canada together, without mentioning any of our problems. We just pretended everything was OK, ignoring the bad things as if they had never happened, as if they weren't *still* happening.

I tried to have fun on the trip, but always at the back of my mind was the thought that we couldn't carry on like this forever.

One day, back at home, we had yet another row. It was about the usual stuff – about how Micky was seeing someone behind my back – and suddenly, I noticed that her eyes weren't right. Her speech had also become slurred, as if she'd been drinking heavily.

I became very worried very quickly. "What's wrong?" I asked, almost too scared to hear the answer.

"Nothing," was the only reply I got.

I wasn't letting it go that easily, however. "There's something wrong, I can tell; you don't look right."

After a few more minutes of denial, Micky finally admitted to me that she'd taken an overdose.

Petrified that she was going to die, I rushed her to Lewisham hospital, and after waiting for what seemed like hours (all the while with horrible thoughts going round my head, of the doctors calling me into the room to tell me she'd died), I was finally allowed into the cubicle to see her.

She was OK. They had pumped her stomach and were going to keep her in overnight for observation. She looked absolutely dreadful but at least she was here, alive, with me. I didn't know what I would have done if she hadn't made it, and the relief that washed over me when I saw she was awake was incredible.

That relief soon vanished.

As I looked at her, I couldn't help but ask her, "Why? Why, Micky? Why do this to yourself?"

At first she didn't reply; she just stared past me, clearly in her own little world.

I tried again. "Please tell me."

This time she did reply, but it was in a voice so faint that at first, I thought I'd completely misheard her. "I want to be a man," she whispered.

I didn't know what to say. What *could* I say? I just sat there in silence, stunned, until she spoke again.

"I knew you wouldn't understand, but I've always known that I was supposed to be a boy." She shrugged, tears threatening to fill her eyes. "I just can't live like this anymore."

I continued to sit there in silence, my mouth wide open. It was taking a while to take in what she was telling me, taking my brain a while to process her unexpected words.

"Say something," she said, and the look on her face almost broke my heart.

I gathered my thoughts. "You need to see somebody about this."

Micky shook her head. "But you'll leave me!"

I took a deep breath, not really knowing what was about to come out of my mouth but knowing I had to say something to try to comfort her. "Listen Micky, if you don't talk to someone about this then you'll only go and do it again. You have to sort it out; if being who are now is making you *this* unhappy, you have to do something. I mean, you tried to kill yourself! You can't go on like this."

I had no idea where these words of wisdom were coming from, but I did know that this was something she needed to do.

I also knew that she was right; I wouldn't be able to stay. After all, I wasn't interested in men sexually, but she didn't need to hear that right now.

The feel of the blade on my skin eased a little of what I was feeling, but not much. *Everything* was going to change, and there was absolutely nothing I could do about it.

Was it me? Was I doomed to spend my life being punished in some way? Was it because of what I allowed *him* to do to me?

Thoughts of his body pushed up against mine flooded through me, making me feel sick and light headed.

49

Trying to block out the memories, I cut again.

***

The next few years were spent visiting psychiatrist after psychiatrist, sitting in waiting rooms while Micky told them how she felt, or while she had another series of tests.

It seemed like it was never ending, but eventually the talking stopped and Micky was put on a course of testosterone, injecting himself daily in order to lower his voice and create more body hair, and I watched – as if in some sort of dream state – as the change started to happen in front of my eyes.

Micky had always been butch looking, but to witness the transformation as the voice deepened and the whiskers began to appear – along with chest hair – was incredible. It was as if I were seeing a complete rebirth. Although I was scared of what it meant for us, it was fascinating to see.

I had to get used to calling her a he, as well as accommodating the considerable change in mood variations, which was a side effect of the testosterone. I stood by him during his transformation, but even while all this was going on, he still had affair after affair, cheating on me while I waited up for him to come home.

Although I knew our relationship had taken on a very serious different dimension, I still felt as though I wouldn't be able to make it on my own; I was just so used to what we had.

So, we stayed this way for several more months, him going out with other people, and me pretending that I didn't know.

After about a year of being on male hormones – in which time Micky had grown a full beard and had become very hirsute all over his body – it was time for him to go into hospital for his double mastectomy.

This operation took place in Manchester, and I booked a room in a local B&B so I could be close by. According to the surgeon, everything went well, and when he came round with the nurse to change Micky's dressings the next day, I saw the aftermath of the surgery.

Even though I knew what he'd had done, it still shocked me. I thought to myself, 'How can anyone have their breasts removed voluntarily?' I realised then how desperate Micky must have felt in all of the years leading up to this moment, as he was more than ecstatic with the results.

He finally had what he wanted. He could finally be happy with himself.

That night, back in my dingy B&B room, I knew that we had come to the end of the road, and I thought about it for hours, before finally making up my mind: I'd stay with him until he recovered, but it was over now, for good.

I had to move on with my life, and so did he.

Leaving

I took care of Micky while he was recovering, but I felt that our relationship had definitely changed by now, and I knew that he felt the same.

Even though I knew it was over, when he was well enough, he suggested a trip to Florida – perhaps in the hope that we could rekindle what we once had – and I agreed. I knew this would be the last holiday I ever had with him, so I wanted to go for that reason, but I was also concerned about the pressure I'd be under when I was alone with him, so I invited my niece, Ruby, along for the second week. I knew it would be a make or break fortnight, and I wasn't sure I could handle it all on my own.

The holiday itself was wonderful – the sun shone down on us and the warmth seeped into my bones, making me feel better than I had done in a long time. In terms of our relationship, while we were on holiday it felt like Micky and I were old friends. It was great, and I hoped that when I left, this would make the situation a bit easier for both of us.

When we returned to England, things went back to how they'd been before, not unsurprisingly. The holiday had been brilliant, but it hadn't done what Micky had hoped. We were definitely not going to get back what we had.

One day, I was visiting a friend on the Ferrier Estate with one of my sisters when a woman walked into the kitchen where we were having tea.

She was stunning, and I immediately felt some sort of attraction to her – not something that happened every day.

"This is Daisy," our friend said, and we all sat around the table chatting about various subjects.

Eventually, we got onto the topic of children, something which was very close to my heart – I'd previously paid privately for donor insemination, which had failed.

"I have three kids," Daisy said, looking at me. "How about you, Michelle?"

A bit uncomfortable, I replied, "None yet. I'd love to have kids, but it's a bit more difficult for me – I'm a lesbian."

Laughing, Daisy retorted, "I couldn't be a lesbian, I like cock too much."

We all joined in with the laughter, but I felt like a deflated balloon. There was just something about her, and I wanted to find out more.

***

I would occasionally meet up with Daisy at my friend's house for tea, and I didn't know if I was reading the signs wrong or not, but there definitely seemed to be something there, like some sort of undercurrent travelling between us. Of course, I thought that it was probably just wishful thinking on my part.

Anyway, a few months passed and then one night, a group of us – including Daisy and my sister, Lydia – went to a local pub for a hen night. Although it really wasn't my scene, I wanted to go out and have fun with the girls, and I'm glad I did.

This was the night that the relationship between Daisy and I changed.

For most of the night, I sat at the rear of the pub, while the rest clambered around the front, where naked men were gyrating on stage. Needless to say, this wasn't exactly the height of entertainment for me, but the atmosphere was great and the alcohol was flowing.

By the end of the evening, Daisy was so intoxicated she could barely stand, and after a few cabs were called for the others, I got into the car with her and Lydia.

When we reached the Ferrier Estate, Daisy informed me that she was locked out of her house, and as her partner would be asleep in bed, she needed me to climb through her living room window, which was unlocked.

Telling my sister to go home and that I wouldn't be long, I propped Daisy up against the front door and went round the back to climb inside. Well, I slid the window along and had my body halfway through when I noticed Daisy's partner, Peter, sitting on the sofa, staring at me.

Feeling incredibly stupid, I muttered my apologies as I let myself into the room. I started rambling about how I thought no one was up and that Daisy was locked out, getting more and more embarrassed by the second.

"Don't worry," he said. "She's always like this when she's had a drink."

I gave a little grimace in reply and then went to let Daisy in, talking to her through gritted teeth. "Peter was sitting on the sofa. I thought you said you couldn't get in? I feel so stupid."

"Oh fuck," she replied. "Is he still up?" With that, she stumbled up the stairs and almost fell into the living room. Swaying on the spot, she shouted at Peter, "Why you still up?" She then proceeded to pick an argument with him, his response to which was to go on up to bed, leaving us alone.

"Well, I guess I'll go," I said, still slightly embarrassed.

Daisy was shaking her head. "No, don't go yet! Stay and have a fag with me."

So, I sat on the sofa while she crawled across the floor to light a fag on the fire, and then we talked about the hen night and my mortification at seeing Peter as I climbed through the window.

It was easy and comfortable to talk to her, and when we both started to giggle, Daisy leaned forward and kissed me on the lips.

Although I was delighted, I pulled back from the kiss. "You're drunk; you'll regret this in the morning."

"Oh, come on," she replied. "You must know what I want."
She kissed me again, and although I considered pushing her away, I
really didn't want to.

So, we continued kissing on the sofa for about half an hour
until I remembered that Micky was meant to be meeting me at
Lydia's, where we were both going to stay the night.

"I have to go," I told Daisy, "and believe what I say – you'll
regret this in the morning."

I left then, and when I got back to Lydia's house, Micky was
already asleep.

I lay awake for hours thinking about what had happened, and
even though I knew Micky and I were over – and even though I
knew he cheated on me – I still felt awful about the whole thing.
Actually, I was experiencing a weird mix of emotions: I felt bad
about what I'd done, but excited as well. It had finally happened
with Daisy!

In the morning, Micky went off to his mother's house, Lydia
went shopping, and I was just lying down on the sofa with a huge
hangover and an Alka-Seltzer when there was a knock at the door.

Once I'd managed to get up and traipse over to open it, I saw
Daisy standing there, smiling at me.

"I came over to see how you were feeling," she said, and I
invited her inside.

We sat there chatting generally, purposely skirting around
what had happened the night before, and the only thing I could think
of was that I was right: she had obviously been very drunk and now

she wanted to forget about the whole thing. Although I'd been expecting this reaction, it still made me sad.

We'd been talking for about an hour when Lydia came back from shopping, and Daisy took that as her cue to leave. "Better get back to the kids."

I walked her to the door and before she turned to leave, she set her eyes on mine. "Oh, by the way, Michelle…"

She hesitated, and I just looked at her, waiting for her to continue.

"I don't regret last night." With that, she smiled and walked away.

I felt the same emotions I'd been feeling the night before – I was completely elated that she felt the same way about me as I did about her, but I also felt incredibly guilty because of Micky.

The more I saw Daisy, the more our relationship blossomed and the guiltier I felt. Even though Micky had cheated on me many times before, it was a new thing to me, and thinking about Micky's infidelities didn't make me feel any better about my own.

After a few weeks of grabbing moments here and there when we could, I knew that my relationship with Daisy had reached a whole new level. We talked about it, and we decided that we wanted to be together properly, as a real family.

After much discussion, we both decided to tell Peter and Micky that it was over. It was a huge thing to do, but we simply had to do it.

Daisy left to go home and wait for Peter to come in from work, and I left to go and see Micky where he was working at the time, painting a house.

Micky seemed genuinely pleased to see me, which of course, didn't make what I was going to say any easier.

"What you doing here?" he asked, a smile on his face.

With butterflies in my stomach, I did my best to keep my voice level as I replied. "I need to talk to you in private. Can we sit in the car?"

Micky looked at me with confusion, but he agreed and we walked to the car, Micky sitting in the driver's seat, with me next to him in the passenger's seat.

Taking a deep breath, I started talking. "Micky, you know things have changed since you had your operation, and we've got to be honest – even before that, things weren't good." I took another deep breath. "I think we should call it a day and go our separate ways."

Micky immediately tried to talk me out of it. "No! We can work it out, we'll be OK, we just gotta give it time!"

I kept my voice even, not wanting to get dragged into an argument. "Micky, it's over. We both know it. I'm just not happy anymore."

Micky wouldn't listen; he just continued on with all the reasons why we should stay together.

He talked until my head spun, and in the end I just screamed out, "I've met someone else!"

The car went deadly quiet, and a while passed before Micky spoke again. "Who is it?"

"It doesn't matter who, but I love her. You knew this wasn't going to work out between us; too much has changed."

He turned to look at me, suddenly shouting, "It's Daisy, ain't it? You've been spending all your time at her house!"

I looked Micky in the eyes, not wanting to lie to him. "Yes."

I didn't think he'd react well to this, but I definitely didn't expect what happened next.

Without waiting for me to say anything else, he started the car and pulled away, driving around the narrow streets at breakneck speed. He drove like an absolute maniac, barely missing other cars and not stopping at give way signs or slowing down for bends.

I honestly thought I was going to die.

"Don't leave me!" was all he kept saying, over and over again.

All I could think of was that I had to slow him down, or convince him to pull over – anything to prevent the inevitable from happening if he kept up this speed. "We can talk about it," I heard myself saying, "but not if you're going to kill us both! Take us back, Micky, and let's talk."

He seemed to contemplate this for a few moments, and finally, he slowed down and returned to where he'd been working.

As soon as the car pulled over to the kerb, I jumped out, screaming at him, "You idiot! You could have killed us both!"

Micky was distraught. "I'm sorry, but I can't lose you."

By now, I was livid. "It's too little too late, Micky. Remember all those times you cheated on me? Went off leaving me, not knowing if you were dead or alive? The sex change? It's over! Too much has happened. We've both changed. We have to move on."

With that, I got back in my own car, tears burning my eyes. I didn't want to hurt him like that, but I knew that I'd done the right thing.

I'd done the only thing I could do.

A Fresh Start

After I left Micky, I took a few items of clothing – just enough to get me through – and went to stay with my sister. Even though I'd left, however, I couldn't get rid of Micky that easily; he kept calling me, begging me to come back and threatening suicide if I didn't.

It was hard to hear him like that, but I knew that I had to stay strong. That chapter of my life was well and truly over, and my new life with Daisy was just beginning. It was incredibly exciting.

Not long after, Daisy rang me to let me know how it had gone with Peter.

"What did he say?" I asked, nervous but wanting to know the answer.

Daisy sighed. "He stood up, he sat down… he stood up again, sat down again… then he told me we should move away and start again somewhere else. He thought that if we did that, things would be better. Then he got angry with me, telling me I wasn't taking the kids and calling me some choice names. I'm not sure if it's really sunk in yet, or if he just thinks it's some sort of phase I'm going through."

It was about what I'd expected really. "So what happens now?"

Daisy replied instantly. "I've asked him to leave. I've just got to give him time to get his head around everything."

I agreed.

Things were hard in the beginning. First of all, Peter told Daisy that she couldn't live in the home they'd shared together – he was going to live there, as he hadn't done anything wrong, and he wasn't prepared to leave. So, Daisy and I moved in with one of my nieces, who also lived on the Ferrier Estate.

Peter then took the kids to Ireland to visit his parents, but after a while he brought the youngest back; she missed her mum drastically, and wanted to be with her. Once he'd dropped her off at ours, he returned to Ireland, where their two sons were still staying with their grandparents.

Daisy had several difficult phone calls with Peter, during which he repeatedly told her that he wasn't going to bring the kids home. On hearing this, she became very down and depressed – she just missed her children so much.

I wanted to comfort her, wanted to make her feel better. I just wished I could magically make this whole situation – and all the pain that had come from it – go away. "Listen," I said, "if he doesn't bring the kids back, then we'll just have to go to Ireland and get them ourselves. He can't do this; it's just his petty way of getting back at you."

By now we had moved into temporary accommodation, after explaining what had happened to the local council. This shelter was in Seven Sisters Road, London, and it consisted of a room with a double bed and bunk beds, plus a shared kitchen and bathroom. This is where we took her daughter on her return to stay with us.

In the end, we didn't have to resort to going to Ireland to get her two sons back. About a week later, Daisy got a phone call from an old friend of hers, who told her that Peter had come back to London, and had left the two boys with a mutual friend.

As soon as Daisy got off the phone, we left to go and get them, and she couldn't wait to bring them back to where they belonged.

When we got to her friend Petra's house, Daisy knocked on the door, clearly brimming with nervous excitement.

When Petra opened the door, she looked at us and said, "I told Peter that if you came, I wasn't going to stop you taking your kids."

Daisy just replied with a simple, "You couldn't."

Then, Petra called the boys to the door and when they saw their mum, they ran into her arms, clearly delighted to see her. The three of them stayed like that for a while, Daisy giving her two sons all the kisses and cuddles that they'd missed while they'd been in Ireland.

Now that there were five of us, the temporary room we were staying in wasn't very practical, so we immediately went back to the local council and were given a private house to stay in until a permanent residence became available.

Relations with Peter at this time were understandably very tense, but soon he found a new girlfriend, Marg, and the whole situation got much better. He finally understood that he could see the kids as often as he wanted, and that I was in no way a threat towards him – he was still their dad and always would be.

One day, something happened that would change our situation again.

Peter had been drinking in a local pub – the 'Wat Tyler' on the Ferrier Estate – when he was violently attacked by a man with a mace on a chain, due to an argument the two had had a few months before.

Peter's injuries from this attack were pretty severe, and there was a chance that the man would come back and attack him again. Things were looking bleak.

After mulling it over, I told Daisy that they could stay with us – him, his girlfriend, and her kids – until the council rehomed them.

Daisy was incredibly grateful, but understandably wary. "Are you sure? I know how awkward this is for you."

I was sure. "He's the kids' dad. How would they feel if they knew he got hurt and that I could have helped prevent it?"

So, they all came and stayed with us, and the animosity between us slowly began to diminish. After a while, Peter and Marg got rehoused into a different area, and they left us to go their own way.

At least some good had come out of this whole mess – our relationship had greatly improved.

I Want To Be A Mum

I had always wanted to be a mum, and after two failed attempts at a private clinic, the longing still remained. I spoke to Daisy about my desire and we agreed to go and visit the GP together to see if he could help.

This GP referred me to King's College Hospital, an institution which inseminated not only straight women, but also same sex couples using donor sperm.

At our consultation with one of the doctors at King's College, we were told about how the procedure worked. "What we do," she said, "is take down a list of characteristics you'd like to have matched to the donor – such as height, hair, eye colour, skin colour etc. – and then we would try to find a donor that matches these characteristics as much as possible. You would then be asked to do an ovulation test, and when you receive a positive result, you need to call us up and make an appointment. Then it will be time for you to come in and be inseminated."

It all sounded good, and I was extremely excited and eager to start. "How long will it take?"

The doctor smiled. "First you'll have to see a psychiatrist, just to ensure that you understand everything and that you're of a stable character. Then, once the report comes back, we can begin!"

Daisy and I got an appointment to see a psychiatrist within a fortnight and as we left the hospital, we were on cloud nine.

"I so want this to work," I said to Daisy. "Being a lesbian doesn't take away the yearning to be a mum." Of course, there were other ways I could have got this done – I could just sleep around until I got pregnant – but that simply wasn't something I was prepared to do.

Daisy hugged me tightly. "This will work. You'll see; you were meant to be a mum."

After my meeting with the psychiatrist at the hospital, we waited for the call from the assisted conception unit, and when this came and I was given an appointment to go and see the consultant, Daisy was as overjoyed as I was. We just couldn't wait.

So, we returned to King's College, where I filled in a form noting down the characteristics I wanted from the donor. I chose blond hair, blue eyes, and between 5 foot 10 and 6 feet. I was told that a lot of the donors were actually student doctors, who used the money paid to them for their donations to put them through medical school. Of course, I was delighted to hear this – good looking and brainy! What a brilliant combination.

I was then given the ovulation prediction test and told to call when I had a positive reading. It was really happening now, and I was getting more and more excited by the day.

Back home, I waited impatiently for my period to come. Once this happened, I could start the fourteen day wait that was needed before I could begin to use the ovulation test.

When I got a positive reading – which meant I was due to ovulate within 72 hours – I ran down the stairs to Daisy, not wanting to miss a single second.

"It's time," I said, my heart thumping away rapidly in my chest.

Looking at the test, Daisy broke out into a huge smile. "Let's ring the hospital."

This is what we did, and the consultant told me to go in the next morning. Even though it was less than 24 hours, it seemed like forever, but I couldn't wait to get started.

The next day, I was full of excitement on the journey to the hospital, and when I got there, I was told to lie down on a bed, which was tilted back slightly to allow the sperm to be placed inside me.

The thought of the sperm itself actually made me feel sick – it brought back all the memories of that dark time of my childhood, and thinking of the taste of salt, I actually gagged.

Within minutes, however, the procedure was over, and I was told to go home and wait to see if my period came.

The wait was agonising. I knew this could be the start to a whole new part of my life, and the thought of what this meant thrilled me to the core.

The other thing I had to worry about was the cost; only this first attempt was free, and so any further treatment would have to be paid for. Unsurprisingly, procedures of this sort were extremely expensive, so this was really our only shot. No pressure, then.

I know it sounds strange, but around a week and a half after the insemination, I felt myself change. I can't really describe how I knew, but I was absolutely convinced I was pregnant.

It was a few days before my period was due, but I couldn't wait any longer: I decided to do one of the two tests I'd bought. A few minutes later, I was sitting in the bathroom, too scared to look at the little stick in front of me. After all, that little stick held my destiny – my future with Daisy, our own little family.

A couple more minutes passed and eventually I plucked up the courage to look at the stick.

There it was.

Or was it?

Was I really seeing a little blue line or was it just wishful thinking?

Shaking my head and closing my eyes, I took a deep breath and then looked again. No, it was definitely there: the blue line that told me I was going to have a baby.

Without wasting another second, I ran down the stairs screaming, "Daisy! I'm pregnant! I'm pregnant!"

She ran up to me and examined the test closely, clearly not wanting to get her hopes up until she'd seen it with her own eyes. After a few seconds, she looked up at me, with the biggest smile I'd ever seen on her face. We fell into each other's arms then, jumping and crying with joy.

I couldn't believe it. All I had ever wanted in my entire life was growing inside me, and I couldn't be happier. Neither could my family; everyone – especially my mum – were ecstatic, something which made me feel even happier still.

Now that I knew I was actually pregnant, the one thing I couldn't wait to find out was the sex of the baby. I felt like once I knew that, I could really start planning for this child.

Of course, the most important thing was that the baby was healthy, and I went for my first scan as soon as possible. The consultant said to me, "Because you're so early, we may not see much at this stage," and as she scanned my tummy, I held my breath, just hoping like mad that everything was going to be OK.

The doctor's voice brought me out of my thoughts. "Look there, do you see that little light flashing?" I looked, realised what she was pointing at, nodded. "Well, that's the baby's heart."

Tears immediately filled my eyes. There was a child inside me – an actual child – and right there was its little heart, beating away, filling me with hope and wiping out a lot of the misery I'd suffered through in order to get to this day. I felt whole, complete, for the first time ever. I remember that day well.

The next scan (at 20 weeks) soon arrived, and there I was again, waiting with baited breath to find out if everything was OK. This scan was even better than the first, because not only was everything fine, but I also found out what sex the baby was.

The doctor focused on the screen and then said, "It looks like a little girl." I cried again with happiness, feeling the unconditional love I already had for my little daughter coursing through me and threatening to spill out of me completely. It was overwhelming – I never thought I could be so happy.

Unfortunately, this happy feeling didn't last too long, as it was around this time that something else happened – something that would shake me so hard I would feel there was never any good to come out of this world.

What happened was this. I was at home one day watching TV with Daisy, my hand resting on my bump, when the phone rang. I picked it up, but at first I couldn't make out who it was or what they were saying, it was so rushed, so garbled.

After a few seconds, I realised it was my niece, Marie, and she didn't sound good.

"Slow down a bit! Marie, is that you?"

I could hear sobbing at the other end of the line, and then her voice came through, clearer this time but still panicked. "I've been raped, I've been raped!"

I immediately felt sick, a deep, clawing feeling in the pit of my stomach. Had I heard her right? "Marie, where are you? Tell me and I'll come and get you."

"I don't know!" she cried, the desperation in her voice breaking my heart. "They raped me."

I tried to ignore those words, knowing that I'd break down otherwise, and knowing that Marie needed me. "Marie, calm down, honey. Please look around you, what do you see? Is there a street name or anything?"

"No," she replied, crying harder now. "There's a black taxi coming," she stammered.

With that, the line went dead.

Now out of my mind with worry, I tried to explain to Daisy what was going on while at the same time dialling the police.

They soon answered, and I yelled at them down the phone, "Hello police! My niece has been raped, and I don't know where she is or what to do!" I could feel the bile rising, burning the back of my throat. I didn't think I'd ever been so angry. In my state of panic, I didn't hear exactly what the police said to me, but I gave them my address and understood that they were on their way.

Nothing happened for about half an hour – half an hour that I spent alternately panicking and trying to keep calm for the health of the baby.

Eventually, I heard a car pull up outside, and I yanked open the door frantically, thinking it would be the police. Instead, it was Marie I saw standing there, a haunted look on her face. I took in the bite marks on her shoulder and the wet patch between her legs where she'd wet herself, and the sight of these things nearly drove me to my knees.

Trying to keep it together, I ran out of the house and hugged her right there while she sobbed into my shoulder. I'd never seen her like that, and it was a very hard thing to get my head around.

A few moments later, the police arrived, and through her sobs we managed to find out that Marie had been pulled into a car, where three men had raped her, taking it in turns. Once they were finished, they left her in an old car park near Peckham, treating her like some piece of meat, which they'd discarded once they'd had their fill.

I felt physically sickened, and so angry I can't even describe it. I wanted to find these men and kill them – make them suffer the way Marie was suffering, and the way I'd suffered in silence as a child. More than anything I wanted to be able to take her pain away for her, but of course, I couldn't.

The police then left with Marie, taking her to a rape centre where a rape kit would be taken, and it was up to me to phone my sister Sharon, asking her to meet them there.

All I could keep thinking was: Marie, my wonderful, lovely Marie! Why was there so much evil in this world? How could those men do this? What was wrong with them? And to do it to such a soft, friendly, lovable girl like Marie.

That night, the nightmares were tenfold. I dreamed he was grabbing Marie and taking her with him to the pit of his depravity, swapping me for my niece.

I awoke knowing she would never be the same again.

***

On the 18th August 1996 at 4.18 a.m., my little girl came into the world: Demi-Marie Eades. The labour was long and painful but I would absolutely do it all again, because it gave me the most precious gift I've ever received. She weighed a perfect 6 lb and came out with a mop of dark hair on her head.

I immediately felt overwhelming love and protection for my daughter, and this feeling shook my body to the core. I swore there and then that I would never ever let what happened to me happen to her; no one would ever hurt her, and no matter what she had to tell me, I would always believe her. Nothing she could say would take her away from me. She was absolutely perfect and she would always be that way to me.

You And Me, Kid

Although I had my beautiful daughter, things with Daisy weren't going too well. It wasn't one big thing, or something either of us had done – in fact, we were both to blame. Whenever we argued, I would always have a nasty, smart mouth, pushing Daisy to sometimes lash out at me. I would retaliate and the arguments would become more physical as we went on. It wasn't good.

Other areas of our relationship were falling apart as well. We hadn't slept in the same room for a few years, and as Demi got older and the arguments escalated, I left the house a few times, unable to cope. I'd always go back, however, hoping that maybe this time we'd be able to work things out and become a family again.

One day, everything changed. I was having yet another argument with Daisy, a particularly nasty one that was beginning to get physical, and I heard the sound of someone sobbing. Demi. I always tried to protect her from witnessing mine and Daisy's fights, but this time she'd heard the shouting from outside the bedroom door and we'd frightened her – she was lying on the bed, crying her eyes out. I picked her up, trying to soothe her, and that's when I knew: I would have to leave Daisy for good. I couldn't keep putting my daughter through this. After all, I wanted the best for her, a good childhood unlike my unhappy one, and all these arguments and fights weren't helping.

Once I'd made the decision, everything moved relatively fast; the council rehoused me and my daughter and we started on the next phase of our journey on our own.

It was a scary and unsettling time. After all, Daisy and I had been together for ten years – not something you can get over quickly. I think it was worse for Demi. She hadn't made the decision to leave, I had, and it was difficult trying to explain the situation to her in a way she'd understand. She hated me for leaving Daisy, as no matter what had happened between us, Demi still loved Daisy – she was like her second mother.

After a while, as time went on, she got more used to the idea of leaving Daisy, and of it being just me and her. The lack of arguments must have been a big part of it – it was a blessing not to be fighting with someone every day.

"You can still see Daisy," I explained to her. "Just because we don't live with her anymore doesn't mean she'll stop loving you." I tried to reassure her as much as I could, but to be honest, it was me who needed the most reassurance.

Although I knew that leaving Daisy was the right thing, it was still incredibly difficult, and I didn't know how to cope with it. The first few weeks of being on my own brought back all my old anxieties – ones I hadn't had for a long time – and once again, the nightmares started. I would wake up sweating and shaking, feeling his hands grabbing me as I drifted from sleep into wakefulness.

Each night the nightmares got worse, and after each one, the need to slice the memories away returned. I wanted so badly to get a knife and cut out the pain, but I couldn't do that anymore; I simply couldn't use it as a coping strategy, not now that I had Demi to look after. So, after much thought, I plucked up the courage and went to see my GP.

My doctor listened to me carefully, then asked, "What brings on these anxiety attacks? What exactly are the nightmares about?"

I explained that I'd suffered from these horrific dreams for many years, and that one of my ways of coping was to self-harm – that is, until my child was born.

He pressed on. "Can you remember what the nightmares are about, Michelle?"

What a question! I averted my eyes and said, "I can remember as clear as if I were there right now."

He continued to look at me, waiting for me to continue.

After a few more seconds of silence, I couldn't take it anymore. "Don't ask me to tell you what they're about, please. I just can't."

The doctor, however, wasn't going to let it go that easily. "Did something happen to you, Michelle?"

At this, I looked him straight in the eyes, and with more venom in my voice than I meant, replied, "I was abused as a child, OK?" I said this through gritted teeth, not believing I was telling him at all and wanting to just get it over with. "And before you ask, it wasn't my parents or my brothers or sisters." I paused. "I'm not saying any more."

The doctor continued to look at me. Not in a horrible, probing way, but with concern on his face, which seemed even worse. Under his caring stare, I almost gave into the tears that were threatening to burst out at any minute.

After a while, he smiled at me. "I'm going to give you something to help take the edge off what you're feeling. It will take some time to kick in, but in the meantime, I would like to refer you for some psychotherapy sessions."

I froze at the word 'psychotherapy'. "No!" I shouted, before lowering my voice. "I don't want to talk about it to anyone, *please*, Doctor."

After considering this for a while, he reluctantly gave in. I breathed a sigh of relief. I left the GP's office that day with a prescription for Prozac in my hand and a promise to return within six weeks. I felt relieved, like I was finally getting somewhere.

However, this wasn't the magical solution I hoped it would be, and it got to the point where I even tried not sleeping so I wouldn't have to face the nightmares. I was constantly tired, which made it hard to try and paint a smile on my face for Demi. But I had to – I had to pretend that everything was OK, for her sake. She was the most important thing in my world.

Unfortunately, things weren't OK, and soon I had to give up my job (I'd been working as a communicator guide for the deaf and the blind) due to the panic attacks I'd been getting. These attacks became more and more frequent until they seemed to be taking over my life. The worst part was that they could occur anywhere and at any time without any warning, and because of this, I preferred staying close to home, just in case.

Eventually, I had to admit that the tablets weren't working. The yearning to cut was becoming stronger with each passing day, but as this simply wasn't an option anymore, I made another appointment to see my doctor.

I told him that I still couldn't sleep, and that I needed more help. He immediately agreed. "OK, Michelle. I'm going to change your medication, and because of your thoughts of self-harming, I'm going to refer you to Oxleas Mental Health Team to see a psychiatrist."

He said it in such a matter-of-fact way that it sounded wrong. So they were sending me to see a psychiatrist. It just seemed so strange!

I left the surgery that day thinking, 'I'm nuts! They think I'm nuts. That's why I need to see a shrink.' This fact hit me right there and then, and suddenly my heart started to drum against my chest as I looked around me. My head was spinning as I took in all the people in my immediate surroundings. Were they staring at me? They were! And not only were they staring at me, they were whispering about me, pointing at me, laughing about me to their friends. I imagined them saying, "There she goes! That's the girl who's nuts, the dirty whore who let her uncle do all those things to her!"

I had to get away, I had to get home. I had to leave all those accusing eyes behind me, all the whispers and laughter. All I could think was: how did they know? Who told them?

I spent the next few days at home, as I couldn't cope with even the thought of going back outside, not with people knowing my dirty little secret. Just the idea of the whispering and the pointing… it was all too much. So, Demi and I spent the weekend laying new carpet in her bedroom and decorating the walls.

I wasn't sure how I'd be able to leave the house again after that, but I had to. Even though it took all of my will power to do it, I needed to leave. Not just for Demi, but also for my ailing mother, who I was caring for at the time. They both needed me, and I couldn't let them down. That thought was more important than my own worries about leaving the house.

My daughter was my saviour, and if she hadn't been there for me then, I can honestly say I wouldn't be here at all now. Even when I was at my lowest, her cuddles, kisses and unconditional love got me through. She was blossoming into a beautiful, intelligent young girl, and I was so proud that she was my daughter. I was so proud to be called 'Mum'.

Those dark, lonely nights when I tried to keep my eyes open so I wouldn't be taken into that horrific reoccurring nightmare were only made bearable by the knowledge that my lovely little girl was sleeping safely in her bed. She needed me, and I needed her. I could do this for her.

A few weeks later, a letter came with an appointment for me to see a psychiatrist at Ferry View Mental Health Centre in Woolwich. I stared at the letter, a jumble of emotions swirling around within me. 'This is where I get the diagnosis of being completely insane,' I thought to myself, but nevertheless, I was determined to go. I was intent on getting help with the anxiety and panic attacks that were haunting me daily.

The bottom line was that I needed to be there for my daughter, and I wasn't much use to her like this.

Losing Our Minds

Just as I was getting on top of my own problems, my niece was just starting with hers.

After her rape, Marie suffered from a mental breakdown. One day, I heard her talking to herself in the living room, and when I asked, "Who are you talking to?" she didn't reply; she sat there as if she hadn't heard me at all. She just continued her conversation with her invisible listener. It was chilling to see.

After several attempts of trying to get her to reply without any success, I called the doctor and explained the situation to him. He came out to check her over and suggested that Marie needed to be admitted to hospital for treatment.

I couldn't believe it. All I could keep asking myself was, 'Why?' Why us? Why our family? What was so wrong with us that we had to be punished in this way? This horrific, cruel, sadistic way?

Marie had already been through enough, even before the rape had occurred; before that awful incident, she'd been in an extremely violent relationship, which she spoke out about after three years of having the shit beaten out of her by her boyfriend. She'd even given her little daughter Coleen (who was only three years old at the time) to her mother for fear that he'd hurt her as well. It wasn't just fights that got a little physical, like with me and Daisy, but much, much worse. He would torture her, putting cigarettes out on her and getting pleasure from the fact that he was scarring her skin.

Eventually, she'd found the courage within herself to leave him, but when she had, she'd been raped. As if, in some sick, twisted way, it was her punishment for leaving an abuser. And now this, this mental breakdown… what more could possibly happen? What had my family done to deserve all this crap? No matter what we did, and no matter that we were good, decent people, badness followed us everywhere. It just wasn't fair.

We visited Marie at the mental health ward a lot during her stay, and on the first few visits there, she seemed just a shadow of her former self, shuffling around the visiting room and talking to herself, trapped somewhere it seemed she couldn't return from. It was heart-breaking to watch.

They had her on all sorts of medication, with plenty of side effects, such as not being able to keep still, fidgeting, or pacing from side to side.

After a few weeks on this medication, we did start to see some improvement, and soon after that, the old Marie seemed to return. Not the Marie from before the rape, but one that I was at least able to have a conversation with, and get some normal responses from. About six weeks after that, she was released from the hospital and went into supported accommodation, where she could get constant help.

That wasn't the end of her hospital visits, however. They turned into a regular occurrence with Marie, as she'd either take too many, having overdose after overdose, or she would come off her medication altogether. It was constant, like being trapped in a revolving door.

One of the worst things were her auditory hallucinations, which didn't seem to get any better no matter what she tried. She would tell me that they tormented her, calling her fat and that she was worthless, that she didn't deserve to be alive. They would also call me names which she would then relay back to me, telling her I was the enemy and not to trust me. When Marie was on her medication, she would tell me that the voices were still there (they constantly were), but that it was like turning down the volume on a radio. She told me there were two bad voices and one good voice, and although I would urge her to listen to the good voice and ignore the others, most of the time the two bad ones were stronger.

Unfortunately, her recovery was sometimes hampered by the treatment she received while in hospital. I remember one such incident well.

I went to visit Marie when Demi was just a baby in a pram, but when I entered the visiting room and asked the staff if I could see her, they told me she was 'sleeping'. They followed this up with, "We'll tell her you called."

I hadn't come to see her just to be sent away again, so I told them I'd wait and then sat down in one of the chairs. For some reason, the staff didn't seem happy with my response, but they didn't say anything, they just walked back into the office. I noticed that they kept looking at me and whispering to each other, and I just knew there was something wrong – I could feel it, deep in my gut.

After a few more minutes of this, I'd had enough. "Right," I told them. "Go and get Marie."

They exchanged nervous glances, and one of them repeated, "We told you, she's sleeping."

"I don't care!" I said, my voice getting more and more aggressive. "Wake her up and bring her in here. Get Marie. Now!"

At this point, the staff obviously realised I wasn't joking around – and that I wasn't going to leave any time soon – and so they went off to fetch her, clearly still reluctant.

A few moments later, they came back, half carrying and half dragging Marie along the corridor. She was dribbling, and one side of her face was drooping, as if she'd had a stroke. She looked awful, far worse than I'd ever seen her before.

"What have you done to her?" I screamed, panicking.

Marie was the one to reply, although it didn't sound like her normal voice – it was slower, raspier. "They gave me too much medication."

I completely lost it then, angry beyond words. I started screaming and shouting at the staff, demanding to see who was in charge, and they scattered like mice. Soon they were phoning round to try and get someone to come to the ward to speak to me, clearly terrified of what I'd do if they didn't.

In the meantime, Marie was staring at me, scared. "Please take Demi away," she cried, her voice barely a whisper. "They're telling me she's the Devil Child, and I don't want them to hurt her!" Although this was difficult to hear, I could see the shame in Marie's

84

eyes as she said those words – I knew that she loved Demi with all her heart, and it must have been hard for her to tell me that.

Then, Marie turned to the staff. "Take me back to my room!" she ordered, before looking at me. "You'll sort this for me, won't you, Mich?"

"I will," I promised, giving her a long hug. "I won't let them treat you like this."

Soon, Marie was back in her room and the manager had made her way to the ward to see me.

I wasted no time. I let rip about how they thought they could drug up my niece and get away with it. Well, how wrong they were! I said I was going to keep a close eye on everything they did from now on, watching what they gave her, and how much, and checking that they were doing their jobs properly.

The manager listened to what I had to say, then looked down at some notes she was holding. "It seems as if the dose they gave her may have been too strong." She paused.

I couldn't believe what I was hearing. "Too strong? Too fucking *strong*? What does that mean?"

"Well," she continued, clearly nervous, "they were relaxants. So this strength would have caused her muscles to relax a little too much, hence the dribbling and the difficulty walking." She paused again. "It wouldn't have done anything to help with the voices, though."

Now I was angry, far angrier than before. "So you mean to tell me," I said, through gritted teeth, "that Marie would have been lying on that bed, unable to move at all, with those voices screaming at her?"

The doctor stared at me solemnly. "This should never have happened. You have my word that this will be investigated and dealt with."

I wasn't leaving it at that. "Your staff just wanted to shut her up, that's what happened!" I was full-on shouting now. "They can't even be bothered to come out of the office, let alone look after their patients! They just don't care!" I could feel my blood boiling, and before I knew what I was doing, I'd picked up a chair and thrown it across the room. "I'm going to report this! And I'll be watching everything you do and everything you give to my niece from now on!"

I stormed out of the room, out of the hospital, into the fresh air. This was all just too much. I just kept thinking: why are we suffering? My God, what had Marie or I done in our pasts to deserve this? To suffer like this? I went home and cried until I could cry no more.

I reported the incident to PALS (the Patient Advice and Liaison Service) at the hospital, as I said I would, and they told me that they'd investigate the incident and get back to me.

I'm still waiting.

Unfortunately, it wasn't just Marie who was showing signs of having a mental health problem around this time – her brother James seemed to be following in her footsteps. He would accuse members of the family of being in cahoots with people who were plotting against him, like some big family conspiracy. He even stated that we'd allowed these people to bug his flat.

For some reason, James threw a lot of these accusations at me, which was strange considering how close we'd been when he was younger. I just couldn't understand why he was so angry at me, and I would always ask him, "Do you honestly think I would do anything to hurt you, James?"

I asked this on one of the many occasions he came to my door, crying and begging me to tell him the truth – to tell him why I was plotting against him. To answer my question, he said, "You'll make money out of it. You'll be sitting in a big house with a fancy car – that's why you're doing it, and yes, I do think you would." He sighed. "All I want is for you to tell me the truth. I'll forgive you, I promise."

I stared at him, hoping I could make him see. "There's not enough money in this world to make me turn against you, or hurt you in any way. You understand that, don't you?"

He looked at me, hesitant, as if he were fighting a demon inside, trying to recall the closeness we once had. I could actually see the fight in his eyes, and I hoped and prayed that he'd see the light.

Suddenly, however, his eyes went blank, and my heart sank as he stared at me.

"Liar," he said, and walked away.

Now, I had never been afraid of James, not even when he was ranting at me for being involved in this supposed plot against him, but soon, that all changed.

The plot – that was a figment of his imagination – had taken a firm hold, and one day, I received a phone call from him. I hadn't heard from him for a while, as he hadn't been talking to me due to the whole conspiracy in his head, so I was surprised to get his call.

"Hello James," I said as I answered the phone.

"Michelle! Please help me, I've been beaten so badly." He was crying, and my stomach lurched at the sound.

"Where are you?" I asked frantically.

He told me and I sped to Eltham to meet him, worried at what I'd find. As I slowed down to look for him, I saw him sitting on a kerb, covering his face with his hands. 'It must be bad if he's hiding his face,' I thought, as I knew James was a fit, strong lad who could easily look after himself. Seeing him like that, I thought something awful must have happened.

I pulled up next to him and opened the passenger door, yelling at him to get in. Still covering his face, he jumped into the car and I quickly drove off.

"What happened?" I asked, scared of what he would say.

It wasn't his answer I should have been scared of, however.

"Just take me home," he replied, still not looking at me, and I drove him to his flat in silence.

When we got there, he finally turned and looked at me. There wasn't a single mark on his face, no signs of a beating whatsoever.

"What's going on?" I asked, feeling completely unnerved.

"Just tell me the truth!" he yelled. "Why are you plotting against me with them? Why are you bugging my flat? Why are you doing any of this?"

The tone of his voice made me even more nervous, and I took a deep breath before replying. "Look, I can't admit to something that's not true. You're ill, James. You need help. I want to help you."

Taking no notice of my words, he just continued to stare at me.

Eventually, he spoke. "If you don't admit it, I'll jump off my balcony, and my death will be your fault."

I could tell by his eyes that the illness had really taken hold, but I didn't know what I could say or do to make him believe me. It all just seemed so hopeless. If he didn't want my help, how could I actually do anything?

"Wait here," he said suddenly, "I have to get something." With that, he got out of my car and went into the block where his flat was located.

I didn't want to stick around to see what he came back out with, so as soon as he was out of sight, I put my foot on the pedal and got out of there as quickly as I could. This time he'd really scared me, as I had no idea what he was actually capable of, and I didn't want to be alone with him while he was like that.

Once I got home, I rung an out of hours mental health helpline (as I had done on a number of occasions in the past) and reinstated my fears regarding James's state of mind. This time they listened, promising to pay a visit and call me back afterwards.

After a while, the phone call came. "Hello, is that Miss Eades?" the voice asked.

I replied and asked, "Do you agree that he needs help?"

"We went to visit Mr Eades," they replied, "and he had an array of weapons on his bed, including a machete, a baseball bat and a kitchen knife." There was a slight pause before they continued. "He admitted to feeling paranoid and explained that the weapons were for people who were after him. When we asked, however, he couldn't explain who these people were exactly."

I listened to this, fear building inside me with each sentence. *I was one of the people he believed to be after him.* "Are you going to get him into hospital?" I asked.

"No," came the reply. "He refused hospital treatment and he is not in a position where we can section him."

I couldn't believe what I was hearing. "So you're going to do nothing?" I said incredulously. "Even after you've seen him? After you've seen all the weapons he has?"

The voice on the end of the phone hesitated and then said, "Ring us if you have any further concerns." That was it.

Angrier than ever, I retorted with, "He will either kill himself or someone else, and on your shoulders be it!" before slamming the phone down.

A few months went by, and although I didn't see him much or have much contact with him, I knew that James was becoming more and more unwell.

Then, one Sunday, his mum Sharon (my sister) rang me. "I haven't seen James for a couple of days," she said, sounding worried. "He was supposed to pick his laundry up from me on Friday but he never came, and I haven't been able to get hold of him since."

As soon as she said those words, I had a sick feeling deep in my stomach. I didn't hesitate with my answer: "Call the police, now."

My sister also knew how aggressive and unstable James had become over the past few months, and she knew the risks. "He'll go mad if the police kick his door down, especially if he's inside at the time."

"Sharon, he could be lying there, needing help," I continued. "Call the police and then ring me back, please!" I was begging her by this point, but I didn't care; I just wanted to make sure my nephew was OK.

I hung up and waited by the phone for what seemed like hours, not wanting to leave its side in case I missed the call. Eventually, it rang, and when I answered I heard my sister Lydia's voice. She was crying. "He's gone," she said. "James is dead."

I clung onto the phone, not able to do anything else. Had she really just said those words? Was it true? I heard someone screaming and realised it was me. This couldn't be happening, could it?

I don't know how, but I made my way to James's flat, and it was as if I were dreaming. That feeling, however, vanished as soon as I got there and saw the police, who were guarding the door to the block where he lived.

"My sister's up there," I told them. "Her son's dead; let me in!"

I was begging the officer, but he just looked at me sadly. "I'm sorry," he said, "but we can't let anyone in until the police have finished."

So, I waited outside, trying not to think about what was happening in the flat, when Marie's daughter Coleen pulled up in a cab. She tried to run past the officer but I grabbed her and held her close to me, both of us standing in the middle of the car park, holding onto each other and crying. It felt like the tears would never end.

When my sisters Sharon and Lydia finally left the block where James lived, they told me what had happened. As soon as I'd finished speaking to her on the phone, Sharon had called the police as I suggested and they had met her at the flat. Due to James's recent behaviour, they had decided to break the door down and enter instead of waiting. Sharon had trailed in after them.

A lady police officer had entered James's bedroom, and as Sharon had gone to follow her, the officer had stopped her, saying, "Wait there, love." Another officer had then gone into the bedroom and after a few minutes, he'd come out, shaking his head. He'd looked at Sharon sympathetically. "Sorry, he's dead."

Lydia went on to explain that Sharon had started screaming at this point, unable to take in the news. A neighbour had heard this and had taken them in while they waited for the police – it was from there that Lydia had phoned me.

I asked about James and they told me the police had found him lying half under his bed with just his boxer shorts on.

It was such an awful time. We went to visit James at the coroner's office, and Sharon asked if I could go in with her, which I did. The room was dark, as heavy curtains had been drawn over what seemed to be a very large window. Once we were in, the assistant opened the curtains and there, lying on a trolley, was Sharon's son, my nephew, still and cold. The glass window was then slid open so we could reach over to him and give him a kiss on the cheek.

As I leaned over James, my emotions overcame me and I whispered a quick, "Sorry," in his ear. I felt so bad that the help I'd tried to get him hadn't materialised, and sad that he had died hating me, thinking I was somehow plotting against him.

As we left the room, Marie, Coleen and some other family members went in to say their own goodbyes, a few at a time.

The strangest thing happened whilst I was waiting for a cab outside the coroner's office, something which I'll never forget. I was standing with Daisy, as we were still good friends and she'd joined me for moral support, and we were silent, lost in our own thoughts.

That's when it happened.

I could have sworn that I heard James call my name, the word spoken with such anguish and sorrow that goose bumps appeared on my arms. Thinking I was imagining things – which wouldn't be surprising under the circumstances – I asked Daisy if she had also heard it, and was shocked when she nodded her head, a look of disbelief on her face.

Neither of us said anything for a few seconds but then Daisy changed the subject, asking, "Where's that bloody cab?"

We both heard it, and I believe it was his way of saying sorry to me for the distance that had grown between us due to his illness.

"I love you James," I said as I climbed into the taxi.

***

We waited for what seemed like an eternity for the coroner's report on how James had died, but it was pretty much as we expected: he'd taken three times the legal dose of propranolol that his doctor had given him for his anxiety. The autopsy also showed that he had experienced a series of mini strokes, and that these may have been one of the reasons his behaviour had changed so drastically in the last few months of his life.

I wished I could turn back time to when James was a child. You see, something happened to him when he was younger (a story he had told me about often) that I believe affected him very badly for the rest of his life.

He had been sent to boarding school for his naughty behaviour, and while he was there, a friend of his approached him while he was playing pool. He'd told James that he needed to talk to him, and James had said that they'd talk, but only after he finished his game. After several more games of pool, he went to look for his friend to see what he wanted to talk about, and when he couldn't find him anywhere inside he went to search the gardens, where he walked straight into his friend's legs. He'd hanged himself.

James had always blamed himself for this. "If only I'd gone to him when he first asked me," he'd often say, and it would break my heart. He couldn't have known. No one could have known.

It was a tough time for me. I was going to miss the boy who had run away from home because he wanted to stay with his Aunty Michelle, the boy who had travelled down the train tracks, endangering himself just to get to me. This boy, who had so much potential and love to give, was gone. He would never get married or have children or grow old.

The curse on my family was just too much to bear.

James's funeral made it all seem real, and so many people turned up to say goodbye. I miss him so much, every single day, and I can only imagine how my sister feels, losing her son.

This I do know, however; he was and always will be very much loved.

Rest In Peach James Eades, 06/03/74 – 04/01/2004.

Marie's Court Case

The men who had violated Marie had been caught, and a committal had been arranged to see if there was enough evidence for the case to be taken to trial. Soon, it was agreed that there was enough evidence, and the next step was to arrange a date for the Crown Court.

By this point, Marie had already started to show signs that she was suffering mentally due to the unimaginable abuse she'd experienced at the hands of those three men, and I use the word 'men' loosely here – even animals in the wild don't behave how they had.

Well, the day came and I attended the court, but I wasn't allowed into the actual court room itself while the trial was going on. This was because I was hoping to be called in as a witness. After all, I had been the first person to see the heart-wrenching state Marie was in after the gang rape, and I wanted to make sure the truth got put across to the jury.

As we stepped into the court building on the first day of the trial, I was horrified to see the three men who had attacked Marie sitting in the foyer, just talking normally and living their lives, when they should have been behind bars for their inexcusable act against humanity. They were sitting with their lawyers, their girlfriends at their sides. Unbelievable.

Well, of course, as soon as Marie saw them, she ran screaming from the building, unable to cope with even the sight of them. I left her in the hands of other family members and went to see the court usher, asking him if they could remove the men from the foyer as they were intimidating Marie. I was told that they'd find somewhere else for us to sit and they did – a box room, no bigger than what I imagined a police cell to be like. This made me feel like preference was being shown to the accused over the victim – strike one against our legal system.

Marie was incredibly distressed. "I don't know if I can face them again," she said, weeping in my arms.

I tried to comfort her, although I knew my words couldn't make much difference to the hell she was currently experiencing. "You can do this. We're all here with you, honey. Go in there and get your justice!" I just about managed to get this out while tears rolled down my face.

After what seemed like an eternity, Marie went in to give her evidence, and the other family members went to sit in the gallery to show their support. I wish I could have done the same, but the rules were the rules, and I paced up and down outside, waiting to be called in as a witness.

Every so often, someone – my sister or one of my nieces – would come out of the room to suck air into their lungs, sobbing uncontrollably at what they'd had to listen to regarding the depraved acts carried out against Marie.

Eventually, Marie herself appeared, the battle scars of having to relive that day – and in front of so many people, no less – deeply etched onto her face.

I asked the usher when I was going to be called, but before he could reply, Marie's barrister came out with some disturbing news. "The prosecution have brought up something that could influence the jury," he explained. "The trial has been halted and another jury will have to be sworn in. This means we'll have to await another trial date."

I couldn't believe it. I didn't want the trial to be postponed, or for Marie to have to go through it all again on another day, whenever that would be. "What was brought up?" I asked. "Have they done this before or something? Is that what it was?"

The barrister shook his head. "I can't say." He turned to Marie then. "You can go home now. You'll be contacted when another date is set."

As Marie slumped against the wall, it was as if all the life had gone out of her. She was going to have to relive it all again, and through no fault of her own.

I was deeply worried. I didn't think she would be strong enough; every time she talked about the rape, it was like she was being violated all over again – strike two against our legal system.

While we were waiting for the second trial date, Marie's mental health deteriorated even further. She was now a shadow of her former self and she soon turned to alcohol, drinking herself into oblivion daily.

I used to beg her to stop. "Please," I said, on yet another occasion where she'd got so drunk she couldn't get to the toilet and had therefore wet herself, "You're going to kill yourself if you don't stop drinking."

The reply she gave me that day will haunt me for the rest of my life.

"You don't understand," she whispered. "I thought they were going to kill me. I read and re-read the graffiti on that car park wall to try and take my mind off what they were doing to me." I sat there in silence, listening to her while she stared vacantly into space. "They laughed as they took turns with me, as they bit me and pulled my hair out. I didn't think I'd ever see my daughter or you again. I was screaming in my head. I wanted them to kill me, just so it would stop." There were no tears at this point, no emotion from her whatsoever as she continued, "So you see, Michelle, I am already dead."

I am already dead. Those four words terrified me to my very core.

I cried that night and for many nights afterwards, unable to sleep as I imagined poor, sweet Marie suffering at the hands of those animals, wishing they were in the room with me right then so I could ensure they would never hurt anyone ever again. If only.

After a while, the date of the new trial was set, and once again, I accompanied Marie to the court with some other family members. Like the last time, I had to wait outside in case I was called as a witness.

By now, Marie was living with regular auditory hallucinations, and so when she took the stand, her mental health was even more unstable than usual. I was told afterwards that when she gave her evidence this time, it wasn't as strongly as she'd done it before; she stumbled over her words, looking as if she were somewhere else as she couldn't concentrate on the questions being asked. Every question she had to consider put her right back in that car park, back to the horrific event that would change her life forever. How can they expect someone to answer questions like this calmly and normally? It's impossible.

Yet again, I wasn't called as a witness, so I couldn't tell the jury how I had received that harrowing phone call from Marie, or how she had looked when she'd eventually arrived at my home. I wanted to paint a vivid picture in their minds, where it would stay forever, as it had in mine. However, the whole case seemed to favour the perpetrators and demoralise the victim – strike three against our legal system.

The jury was sent out to consider their verdict, but as Marie didn't want to stay inside the court house for even a second longer than necessary, we all went home to await the outcome.

Marie just sat in a chair, motionless, waiting for that call. It was as if she was locked in a world far away from ours, mumbling to the voices that had invaded her head. It hurt me so much that these animals had not just taken her body, but her mind as well. They had to pay for what they'd done to her.

The phone eventually rang, and I picked it up, my heart racing. "Yes?"

"Not guilty," the family liaison officer said.

I couldn't believe it. Had I misheard? I asked her to repeat what she'd said.

"I'm so sorry, but the verdict was not guilty. I don't know what to say. I think Marie came across stronger in the first trial, but I'm just as surprised as you are at the verdict."

I was completely stunned. How was I going to tell Marie that the jury didn't believe her? That she'd gone through all of this – the attack and then the court, twice – for nothing? It was too much to take in.

After a few seconds, I asked the officer, "What was brought up in the first trial that caused another jury to be sworn in?" I thought I knew, but I wanted to make sure. I needed to make sure.

"It was mentioned that in the defendant's car, there was some torn underwear found that didn't belong to Marie," she replied. "It was felt this could influence the jury, as it indicated another person had been attacked in that vehicle."

I slammed the phone down, incredibly angry. So they *had* done it before, to someone who hadn't come forward, and now Marie was suffering for it. She was paying the price. There was so much about this whole case that just wasn't right, not at all.

I don't know how I found the strength to tell Marie of the verdict, that the people who had turned her life upside down were now free to walk the streets, but I did.

101

"So they think I'm a liar?" she asked, with a dark look in her eyes that I hadn't seen before. I nodded, trying to keep the tears in my eyes from falling. "They got away with it?"

I nodded again, watching helplessly as she drank a bottle of vodka until she passed out on the sofa.

My heart ached for her so much it hurt. This lovely girl had suffered so much in her life, from her previous abusive relationship to the horrific incident in that man's car… it had all made her believe she was worthless, and that the beatings were her own fault. She had survived it all, but at what cost? She'd swore she would never put up with any type of abuse ever again, but now she just looked broken beyond repair.

I wished I could help her, I wished I could wipe all of those haunting memories out of her mind like wiping a video tape clean, but I couldn't. I couldn't do anything except hope and pray that somehow she'd be given back to us, and still in one piece.

A few years later, I thought that she'd finally found her happiness, when she met and married a man called Alan. When she walked into the registry office carrying her bouquet, she looked better than she had in a long time. Her daughter, my daughter and a few good friends were there as her bridesmaids, and the rest of the family were also there to celebrate with her.

I was happy for her, but there was one thing that tarnished my happiness: her new husband was also a drinker, and the both of them used alcohol to paper over the cracks that life had left. This wasn't a good mix when you needed a solid wall to lean on, and Marie most definitely needed that.

Still, it was a nice day as we welcomed the new Mr and Mrs Rossam into the family.

Goodbye Marie

In my opinion, not only did the rape have a part to play in what eventually happened to Marie, but the whole trial left a sour taste in everyone's mouths and was also, I believe, partly to blame.

Marie was sectioned on the mental health ward more times than I care to remember, the main reasons for her admittance being several suicide attempts and the fact she kept coming off her medication. I made sure I visited her every day, and I would also get permission for day release so I could bring her home for a while, where she could try and relax in safe and comfortable surroundings.

I remember one occasion that showed me just how well – or not, as it turned out – the nurses were looking after her. It was just after another of her suicide attempts, and she was once again sectioned under the mental health act and put on 15 minute suicide watch. I was just getting ready to leave my house to go and visit her, and as I stepped out of the door, I heard someone call my name. It sounded like Marie.

Sure enough, when I turned round, I saw her running down the road in her nightie, barefoot and looking incredibly distressed.

"What happened?" I asked her.

"I've escaped!" she replied, as she ran past me and into the house. Her hair was unkempt and she had a lost look in her eyes, as if she'd been running from an unseen tormentor, trying to escape some cloak of evil that was chasing her. I tried not to think of my nightmares.

"But why have you escaped?" I asked her. "What happened exactly?"

Her response was, "They're trying to poison me, they all are!"

I sat down with her for at least three hours, trying to calm her down and reassure her that no one was trying to poison her, that I wouldn't allow that to happen.

After three or four coffees and a lot of coaxing, she finally allowed me to call the hospital to tell them where she was.

I dialled the number and waited for someone to pick up. "Hi, this is Michelle Eades, Marie Rossam's aunt."

Before I could say another word, however, the voice on the other end of the phone replied, "Oh Michelle, yes, Marie is fine."

Well, it's safe to say that I was incredibly confused by this response. Did they just say what I thought they said?

I decided to play along and see what would happen. "Good, it's just I haven't been able to get in to see her yet, and with her being on suicide watch, you know how much I worry. How long ago did you see her?"

"About five minutes ago," the voice answered. I couldn't believe it.

"If that's correct," I said angrily, "then can you please tell me how on earth she's been sitting on my sofa for the last four hours in just a nightie and no shoes?"

The voice stuttered, eventually putting me on hold. I could hear muffled voices so she'd obviously just put her hand over the phone's mouth piece, and eventually, another woman came on the line. "I'm so sorry," she said. "There seems to have been a bit of a mistake. We got mixed up with the times we last saw Marie."

"Mixed up with the times?" I yelled down the phone. "She's on fifteen minute obs! For all you know, she could have killed herself!" I took a deep breath, trying to calm down. "I'm bringing her back now."

When I returned Marie to the hospital, I created such a scene that they threatened to call security on me, but after I threatened to go to the papers about what had happened, they couldn't apologise enough for the 'mix up'.

I left the ward with a promise that I would phone every few hours to check up on them, as well as visiting outside of normal hours to ensure Marie's safety. They obviously couldn't look after her without my help, it would seem.

Unfortunately, this wasn't the first or the last time that Marie's illness had led her to believe she was being poisoned. On several occasions, she accused me of putting something in her coffee, and she also thought I was refusing to answer the door when she knocked – she told me she saw me hiding behind the curtain at the window.

During all of these times, I would just hold her, whispering words of reassurance in her ear until she finally calmed down.

This would work temporarily, but the trouble was that Marie didn't really have much to look forward to, and I wanted to give her something positive to focus on, something to be happy about. So, one day I went to visit her at the hospital with a question in mind.

"Marie, would you be Demi's Godmother at the christening?"

She stared at me for a few moments, not saying anything. It was as if she was waiting for me to say, 'only joking,' but I held her gaze, letting her know I meant it.

"Really?" she eventually asked, sounding hesitant. "Even after all those nasty things I said to you about her? You still want me to be her Godmother?" There were tears shining in her eyes.

"Yes," I replied. "I can't think of anyone who loves her more than you do. Apart from me, of course."

By now the tears were falling down her cheeks, and she whispered to me, "I'd love to."

A few weeks later, Marie stood tall and proud at Demi's christening, holding a candle as my daughter was baptised. As I watched my niece, my heart swelled with love and pride for her.

It was a special day.

***

Well, the years came and went, and every so often Marie would get sectioned, which broke my heart over and over again. The worst part was that each time she was admitted to the hospital, we lost just a little bit more of her – bit by bit, she was fading away. It was awful.

It was December 2005 and Christmas was looming – it seemed to be coming around quicker every year, or so it seemed. Marie was due to be released on the 12th, so she'd be home for the festive period, and even after everything, she seemed to be looking forward to it.

In fact, the day before my usual visit, she seemed to be in very high spirits, laughing and joking and eager to get home. She even said she couldn't wait to put up her Christmas tree, which seemed to be a good sign – looking forward to the future, finding hope and encouragement in little things.

There was something that worried me during this period, however; she told me about a dream she had, where James was standing at the bottom of her bed and 'calling' to her.

This immediately worried me, and as gently as I could, I asked, "Marie, you know James wouldn't want you to do anything to hurt yourself, don't you?"

She stared at me for a while before replying, "I know; it was just a dream… but it made me feel safe."

Safe. That was a disturbing word, considering the circumstances. I wanted her to feel safe here, in the real world, but I supposed that wasn't something that was likely to happen.

Anyway, she changed the subject straight away, and soon she was laughing and joking again.

I left that day with the hope that this Christmas would be a good one, even for Marie.

***

Unfortunately, it wasn't meant to be.

"Michelle, is that you?" It was Ruby's voice coming down the phone line, and it sounded urgent, panicked.

"Yes, what's up?" I asked gently, thinking it would be something to do with her dad, Jimmy, who had been ill for a while.

What she said next totally floored me. Just two little words: "It's Marie."

My stomach lurched, and I knew before she even said anything else that it was very, very bad news.

"She's gone, Michelle."

My response was automatic – "Gone? What do you mean, gone?" – but I already knew what she meant. There was a desperate coldness lingering in the depth of my stomach.

"She's dead."

Even though I'd already come to that conclusion myself, I let out an involuntary scream when I heard those words. It took me a while to realise the sound was coming from me.

Ruby waited for a few seconds until I'd calmed down, then asked, "Is Sharon with you?" She could only just get the words out, she was so distraught. I could picture herself sitting there, choking on her tears, and I felt numb.

"Yes," I responded, trying to keep my voice level. "I'll tell her."

After that, I hung up the phone and tried to stay calm. I had to speak to my sister Sharon, and I couldn't break down while delivering the news; I had to try and be strong for both of us.

She almost keeled over when I told her, and I couldn't blame her – both of her children were now gone. At this thought, the coldest of chills ran down my spine. This should never happen to anyone; it wasn't fair.

I just kept telling myself that I had to be strong. I had to see Sharon and the rest of the family through this – there wasn't any other choice.

The hardest part, however, was still to come: we had to tell Coleen, Marie's daughter, about her Mum's death. Just how on earth was I going to find the strength to do this?

As it turned out, she already knew something bad had happened because she'd got a phone call from someone saying how sorry they were to hear about her mother. I couldn't believe it.

Without wasting any time, she called me and asked, "What's wrong with Mum?"

She wanted to know right there and then, but I couldn't tell her over the phone – there was no way. So, I told her I was just five minutes away and that we'd talk once I got there.

Sharon and I drove over straight away, and when I pulled up at the curb, Coleen was waiting at the door.

I needed to go to her and tell her the news and comfort her, but I found I couldn't move; it was as if I was glued to the car seat. I just kept picturing her face as I told her, all the pain and fear and anger that would no doubt cloud her features the second she knew the truth. It was too much.

I was still just sitting there, so Sharon got out of the car and walked over to where her granddaughter was waiting. I watched from my seat as Sharon rested her hand on Coleen's shoulder and leant forward to deliver the devastating news.

The reaction was instant and awful. She screamed – a scream filled with total agony – and it is a sound that still haunts me to this day. Coleen then threw her mobile phone down on the ground and ran inside the house.

Seeing that seemed to wake me up, and I undid my seatbelt before dashing out of the car, running inside after Coleen and finding her in her bedroom. She was lying on the bed, crying.

When I put my arms around her I could feel her sobs vibrating through my body, and I just stayed there with her, rocking her in my arms and trying to say comforting words. "Shh, it's OK, I'm here." I wanted to soothe her, wanted to let her know that she wasn't alone. I wasn't sure if it helped at all, but I didn't know what else to say. What *could* you say in that situation?

After a while, Coleen spoke. "I thought she'd taken another overdose and was in the hospital again. I didn't think…" Her voice broke as she tried to get out the words, and I just continued to hold her in my embrace, wishing I could take all this pain away for her and knowing I couldn't.

Soon, my thoughts turned to my own daughter; I had to tell Demi that Marie had gone to Heaven. How did you tell a nine year old girl that someone close to her had died? Would she even understand what I was saying?

Still, I had to do it, so I arrived at Demi's school and the receptionist brought her to me.

The first thing she asked was, "Have you been crying, Mum?" as she looked at me with those big brown eyes of hers. This was going to be hard.

"Darling, I need to tell you something." The tears I was trying to hold in for her sake started trickling down my cheek, and I took a deep breath before stating, "It's Marie." Trying to pull myself together, I carried on. "You know she hasn't been well for a long time? Well, God could see that and so he's taken her to live with him in Heaven."

She stared at me for a while, then nodded as she said, "I'm doing a play in assembly today, Mum, and I'm going to do it for Marie." Then she kissed me and hugged me before I took her back to class; I believed it was the best place for her to be right then.

After the autopsy had been done, it was disclosed that Marie had taken an overdose of her prescribed drug, carbamazepine, and that this was the cause of death. I was so angry; the very people who'd said she wasn't to self-medicate had given her two weeks' supply on her release and left her to it. Marie had then gone straight to a friend's house and had taken them all in one go. No alcohol was found in her blood, either, so she'd done it stone cold sober.

I mourned her, and I still mourn her to this day, but I knew that she just couldn't take the suffering anymore, couldn't live her life after what it had become. It was very, very sad, but I understood why she did it.

The visit to the coroner's office was harder than I thought it would be; it was like going back in time to when we'd gone to see James. A lump formed in my throat when I saw Marie lying there, her skin as white as the sheet that covered her. It looked like a single tear was escaping from one of her eyes and I cried with her.

Marie's cremation took place on the 4th January 2005, which was somewhat appropriate, as it was a year to the day that her brother James had died. The church was so full on the day of the service that the gallery upstairs had to be opened in order to fit everyone in, and it was nice to see so many people there to celebrate Marie's life.

Coleen picked the songs for her mum's service and the one that escorted us into the church that day was 'Mama' by the Spice Girls. I couldn't look at her as I entered; the pain she was in was just too much for me to bear.

Coleen was so brave; she stood up to give a speech about her mum, and even though she couldn't get all the words out properly through her tears, everyone knew what she was saying. Marie was loved, and she always will be.

Rest In Peace, Marie. Suffer no more xx

The Impact Of Loss

After the funeral, I went around in a complete daze; I just couldn't believe that I wouldn't see Marie anymore. We'd been so close throughout her life that when she died, it wasn't just like I was losing her, it was like I was also losing a part of myself.

I could feel that all-too-familiar black cloud engulfing me, suffocating me as it dragged me down into a dark hole. I felt like I was clawing at the air around me, just trying to keep myself from drowning, but I knew that I had to stay strong for my daughter and the rest of my family.

I didn't want Demi to see me like this, so I asked Daisy to come round and pick her up so that I could have some time to myself to grieve properly. As soon as they were gone, I literally fell into a heap on the floor, rocking back and forth and crying so much I didn't think I'd ever be able to stop. I was begging Marie not to be dead. "Please don't be dead, Marie, please don't be dead." I whispered this over and over like a mantra, hoping that if I said it enough times, it would somehow become true.

That old familiar feeling washed over me then, and I started to picture the blade in my hand, cutting deeply into my skin. I could almost feel the release, all of the pain whistling out of me as I continued to cut. I wanted to do it so badly.

I stayed there for I don't know how long that day, rocking back and forth and silently praying for the strength to get through this without harming myself. After all, I couldn't let Demi see me like that.

The medication I was on at the time wasn't working. I couldn't do anything; I couldn't sleep, I couldn't get up, and when I did manage to get a few minutes of rest, the nightmares still pursued me, chasing me down like they used to.

Around that time, I would just be on auto pilot, getting enough done to take care of Demi but apart from that, not really looking after myself – I didn't even bother to wash myself most days.

Thoughts of suicide flashed through my mind, as I thought that perhaps the numbness of death would be the only thing to take away my nightmares and my pain. Whenever I felt like this, I would go into Demi's room and snuggle against her while she was sleeping, breathing in the smell of her and building up the strength to keep going. I couldn't leave her in this world without me, so I continued to fight the urge to cut. I took my medication and made an emergency appointment with my psychiatrist in the hope it would help.

"Do you have thoughts of killing yourself, Michelle?" the psychiatrist asked me. When I nodded my head – I was crying too much to speak – he continued, "And have you thought of *how* you would kill yourself?"

Taking a deep breath, I nodded again. There was no point in lying.

"What do you think has stopped you from carrying out these thoughts?"

This time, I answered without hesitation. "My daughter. I can't leave my daughter."

It was then that I started to feel incredibly odd. The sound of the clock on the wall got louder and louder, the ticking noise of the hand echoing around my head. At the same time, the psychiatrist's voice seemed to fade away, as if he were walking away from me. The room started to spin, making me feel incredibly sick, and I remember thinking that somehow, it was as if I wasn't there, like I wasn't in the room with the psychiatrist at all but somewhere else entirely. It was strange and frightening, but the feeling left as quickly as it had come.

I soon realised the psychiatrist was staring at me. "You went very pale then, Michelle. Are you OK?"

I tried to explain that I'd gone very dizzy, and that I'd felt like my body had come out of itself somehow. When he asked me to continue, I told him, "I'm not sleeping, I can't eat… everyone is looking at me, pointing at me, talking about me…" I trailed off, not knowing what else to say.

"Do you hear voices?" he asked, a look of concern on his face.

I told him I didn't, "But my thoughts are loud. I know they're just my thoughts but they won't let me rest."

After a few more minutes of talking, the psychiatrist decided that my medication needed changing, so he prescribed me 225mg of venlafaxine and 10mg of aripiprazole. This is actually the same dosage that I take today, and although it doesn't cure my mental health problems by any means, it does take the edge off them enough so I can get through the day.

After her mother's death, Coleen began to drink a lot – she closed her feelings off to the world and tried to dampen them with alcohol. Whenever I saw her, she was either already drunk of halfway there, and I could see the pain written all over her face as her life was spiralling out of control. It was awful to watch, and I tried to reach out to her, to comfort her, but unfortunately the only person who could have done anything to help had been ripped away from our family.

One evening, it all got much worse, and it started with my sister Sharon calling to tell me that Coleen had locked herself in her room, crying. "I've asked her what's wrong but she won't answer me," she continued. "I think she's been drinking and I'm worried about her."

I told her I'd be there in ten minutes, hung up, and jumped in my car. On the journey I tried not to think about what Coleen could have actually done; it was too much to bear.

When I arrived at my sister's house, my great nephew was already there, knocking on Coleen's bedroom door but getting no response.

I said I'd try and I knocked on the door as well, pleading for Coleen to let me in. There was no answer.

I knocked harder. "Coleen," I said, "if you don't answer me I'm going to kick down this door."

I waited a few moments and eventually heard a muffled reply: "I just want to die."

My body felt like it had been hit by a bolt of lightning, as if the air had been knocked out of me. "Coleen?" I shouted, my voice more urgent now, "Have you done something to yourself? Have you taken anything?"

She just replied with, "Leave me alone," her voice barely a whisper.

I knew I had to get in there before it was too late – something inside me sensed that she'd already taken the first step to end her life. I hammered on her door while I screamed at my sister to call an ambulance, more desperate than ever to get inside.

She still hadn't answered when the ambulance arrived fifteen minutes later, and I begged the paramedics to help her. I explained everything that had happened to Marie and how Coleen had been on a downward spiral ever since.

After listening to me, the paramedics went and knocked on the door, shouting that they were there to help and that they wanted to check she was OK. There was no response to any of it.

When it became clear she wasn't going to answer, one of the paramedics turned to me and said, "We can't force her out of there. As she isn't known to mental health, we can't force her to come with us."

I couldn't believe what I was hearing. "What do you mean?" I asked, getting more and more frantic the longer this was going on. "So you're just going to leave her there to die?"

They still refused to help, so I asked my nephew to go and find a neighbour, someone who could help us break the door down.

In the meantime, the police had arrived (after being called by the paramedics), and were waiting outside. One of the officers told me, "If you want her forced into hospital, you'll have to get her outside the house before we can arrest her under section three of the Mental Health Act."

Just then, my nephew came back with a male neighbour, and together they were able to kick down the bedroom door.

We ran inside and found Coleen lying on the bed, empty tablet packets at her side. It was what I feared, but now at least I had the power to do something.

I told my nephew to help me lift her, and together we got her down the stairs and out of the house. She tried to kick and bite us the whole way, but we just carried on, knowing we had to get her outside.

I cried as the police handcuffed her and arrested her under the Mental Health Act, even though I knew it was for the best. I felt as if I was punishing her, but I didn't want to lose her too, and without help, that would no doubt happen. It was as if history was repeating itself, unfolding in front of me yet again. Well, I wasn't going to have that; I would not allow Coleen to be taken from us as well.

In the end, Coleen was in the mental health ward for about a week, which was hard as it was the same ward her mum had been in before her death.

When I went to visit her, she looked tired and somewhat lost, and when I asked her how she was feeling, she just said, "Not too bad."

I told her that I felt awful for carrying her outside so the police could arrest her, but that I couldn't and wouldn't leave her there to die. She just nodded in response.

I knew she had a long way to go and that I'd have to keep a close eye on her, and I made a promise to take care of her – a promise I wasn't going to break.

As Coleen continued to drink herself into oblivion, I constantly told her how much I loved her and how much I would always be there for her, praying that my words would find their way through the muddle in her mind enough to make a difference.

At the same time as Coleen was having her problems, I also had to watch my sister Sharon shrivel to a shadow of her former self in front of my very eyes. Each day of being without her children was harder than the day before, and I could tell that she was carrying around a lot of guilt. As the weeks went by, her mental health also deteriorated until she too was the under the mental health team and she had to rely on medication just to help her get up in the morning. It was devastating to see.

"The hardest thing," Sharon once told me, "is that I'll never be called 'Mum' again."

What could I say to that? As much as I wanted to take the pain away for her, all I could do was be there, through every day and each special occasion that came along – these days just brought back bittersweet memories and the absence of Marie and James was all too obvious. Their lives had been cut short so early, and they'd never again experience another Christmas or birthday – the family would never give or get any Christmas or birthday cards from them again. There was nothing but heartache, and I often found myself thinking, 'Will this pain ease? Would this family ever be able to move on?'

I'm happy to say that things did get better for Coleen, at least. Her time at college finally paid off and she found a job as a veterinary nurse at a local private vets, and although her drinking continued, the employment gave her something else to focus on.

Everything changed again when she fell pregnant, and on the 3rd September 2009, she gave birth to a beautiful baby girl called Chelsey, followed by her son Nathan in May 2011. This is what she needed – someone else to love, and her two children helped heal her in a way nothing else could. Nathan was later diagnosed with autism (along with some other disabilities), but Coleen has taken on the role of Mum with gusto, and I am very proud of her.

Unfortunately, things didn't go quite so well with some other members of my family. The loss of my niece and nephew was still weighing heavy on all of our hearts – and taking its toll on our mental health – when in February 2006, my sister Lydia's husband passed away after a long illness. It was heart-breaking; he was the kindest, softest, most gentle man there ever was.

After being married to the man for almost 42 years (and having had four beautiful children with him), Lydia hit rock bottom, and as she couldn't be left alone after her breakdown, she stayed with me for six months until the doctors found the right medication for her, or at least enough to stabilise her.

I was happy to help her, but as I was spending so much time looking after my family, I ended up ignoring myself and my own needs. Because of this, my mental health also started to deteriorate.

Legacy of Mental Health

All I could keep thinking was: is there something wrong with us as a family?

Did I allow what happened to me as a child to somehow put a curse on the rest of us?

These thoughts still go through my head today; it's hard not to think about the impact all of the mental health problems (e.g. depression, anxiety, panic attacks, paranoia) have had on my family. After all, they seemed to have many of my family members in their uncompromising grip.

Was it a random thing? Was it just coincidence? It didn't seem to make any sense.

Then something happened which made me feel like it was a condition being passed down from family member to family member.

Demi. All I could think was, 'God please, no. Not my daughter, please don't let my Demi suffer at the hands of this unrelenting fog that clouds our minds.' But it was there, I could see it, and it all came to a head one day when Demi heard a piece of news on the radio.

Considering the fact that she wasn't really a fan of Michael Jackson (she never acknowledged his music apart from singing along to the odd song on the radio), I found it immensely strange when his death was announced and I saw my daughter change almost immediately – it was as if something had snapped inside her.

She began putting up posters of him on her bedroom wall, locking herself in her room and crying over him. She would buy anything she could get her hands on that featured his name or his face, and she even started drawing pictures of tombstones on her walls.

I would have understood this more if she'd been a big fan of his, but she'd never shown any interest in him at all when he was alive. I began to wonder if everything we'd been through as a family (her two cousins committing suicide, watching the effect my own mental health was having on me and so on) was now showing itself in her actions. It was as if everything she'd experienced during her younger years had been lurking inside her, just waiting to bubble to the surface, and for some reason, Michael Jackson's death was the catalyst.

I asked her what was wrong and why she was crying over the death of someone she didn't care about, but she wouldn't reply – she'd just carry on sobbing. Soon, her general mood and demeanour began to change; the once bubbly young girl became withdrawn and angry. It was a more amplified version of what happens when girls reach a certain age, but I knew it wasn't hormones that were doing this.

I felt incredibly guilty at the time and I still do. I should have shielded her from everything that was going on, I should have noticed how it was affecting her and I should have paid more attention to her during all the tough times. It was like these problems were my legacy – a terrible gift from mother to daughter. Was this affliction going to follow us until the end of time? It certainly seemed that way.

Not long after, Demi began to suffer from panic attacks which would cause her to walk out of school. I'd have to go and pick her up, and as her anxiety would be so bad, I'd have to drive around for ages just to calm her down.

I tried asking her again what was wrong and she replied that she didn't know. "The attacks come from nowhere," she said. "I feel shaky and scared."

I hugged her until the sobs left her body, by which point she was so exhausted she fell asleep.

It was getting worse; the attacks were happening more and more often and because of this, she was losing a lot of time at school. Getting desperate and not knowing what else to do, I spoke to her head of year, informing her of what was going on, and she referred Demi to the 'best team' where she could go at any time and talk to a counsellor.

I felt better when I knew she had someone to talk to (even if it wasn't me), but I was so very, very wrong to think this.

As it turned out, the counsellor at the best team had a son that taught at the school. He was relaying private information to him and he in turn would approach the students in question, getting them to confide in him. He would then use this trust and take advantage of them, forming inappropriate relationships.

I found out he'd done this to one of Demi's best friends before trying to contact Demi via Facebook, suggesting they go to his house to watch some videos.

I was horrified, and needless to say, the police were called in. It was so frustrating – any good that the 'best team' may have done had now been completely undone.

I spent many nights pacing the floor and worrying about Demi, praying that God would spare her from the trauma of mental health problems. Hadn't she already been through enough?

As well as everything the family had been through, I knew that her not knowing who her father was had affected her deeply. I'd never hidden the fact that she was conceived by artificial insemination, as I wanted to be honest with her from the start.

I remember that first conversation clearly. "I feel like I don't know who I really am," she told me. "I could have brothers and sisters who I don't know about."

I knew she was angry with me for the whole thing, but I didn't want to apologise for the way I'd brought her into the world – what other choice did I have?

She cried as she asked me her next question. "Would you go through all this again if you knew it would make me feel like this?"

As I said, I'd always been honest with her and I wasn't going to change that now, so I replied, "Yes, because you don't know what it's like to yearn for a child of your own. Someone you can love unconditionally and who will love you back." I smiled at her, wanting her to see my point. "When you hold your own child in your arms, you'll understand."

It was clear she was still angry after this conversation, but soon we grew closer, and I knew that she was grateful for my honesty. Because of all this, I dismissed it as being a factor in her own deteriorating mental health, instead looking at other explanations.

I tried everything in my power to make her feel better – I listened while she talked, I was there for her while she cried, and I hugged her until my arms ached, but none of it made any difference, and I think that was the worst part about it for me: I couldn't ease her pain, and it was destroying me inside.

On top of all this, my mum – who Demi had always been extremely close to, ever since she was a baby – had suffered from several strokes and was now bedridden. It was awful to see her like that, but whenever Demi walked into the room, you could see the smile reach Mum's eyes; she was always so happy to see her.

Mum would ask Demi to paint her nails for her, and they would sit together for ages, talking and laughing. Whenever Demi would ask her what nail polish colour she wanted, Mum would reply with, "Ooh, a nice, bright colour. You never know, I might get lucky!"

I would sit and watch them bond like this, feeling the love grow between them, and I was so happy that Demi had her nan in her life.

Like me, my mum was always extremely proud of Demi, telling me, "She'll go far, that one." I smiled, replying that I knew – Demi was incredible.

At this point, I was visiting Mum most days. Even though there was 24 hour care where she lived, I would do as much as I could for her – cooking meals, feeding her, and helping her change position when she was uncomfortable. Whoever went in to visit her would always leave with a smile on their face, guaranteed.

Soon, however, her condition got much worse; as she'd been in bed for so long, she had severe bed sores, and some were so deep you could actually see the bone. Horrified, I contacted social services, and the social worker came and told the staff that they'd have to turn her more regularly, and that they simply had to move her every couple of hours. When she'd gone, I reiterated her message, but with a little more force in my voice; this was my mum, and I wouldn't stand back while she didn't get the care she needed.

I was worried they wouldn't heed the social worker's instructions, as some other things had happened previously which had flagged concern. For example, Mum had been assaulted by a member of staff who'd hit her arm off the bed so hard it had resulted in bruising – her skin was as black as coal.

When that had happened, I'd called the police and the carer in question had been arrested. It had gone all the way to court, but she was found not guilty due to a lack of evidence. I was so angry at this verdict, and from that day on, I made sure that Mum was getting the care she needed, checking up on what was happening and reporting anything that was wrong. After the incident with her arm, there was no way I was going to trust them with her care without keeping a careful watch on all of them.

After she had her third stroke, I went to visit Mum in the hospital and she was completely distraught. She just kept saying to me, "I don't want to die in hospital! Please let me go home!"

It was horrible to see her like that but I was determined for her to get her wish, and after she got over a bout of pneumonia, she was eventually allowed to go home. Unfortunately, she was getting worse; she was becoming more and more confused and she had a severe lack of energy due to not eating enough. She would just sleep most of the day, not eating or drinking or doing anything really, and seeing her like this greatly affected Demi. I wished she didn't have to see her nan like that, but there wasn't much choice.

One evening, I decided to stay with Mum and sleep on the sofa, and in the middle of the night, I heard a noise.

Mum had suddenly sat bolt upright – which she hadn't been able to do for a long time – and was whispering Marie's name. When I went over to her, I asked if she was OK but there was no response; she just kept saying, "Marie" with a smile on her face. She then went on to say, "Of course I've seen your grandchildren; they're beautiful!"

After that, she lay down and went back to sleep, looking more restful and at peace than I'd seen her in a while. I thought of what she'd said, and I truly believed that she was drawing close to all of the loved ones we'd lost over the years. It was nearly time.

A few weeks later, my brother Al stayed over at Mum's like he often did, and on Sunday 15th July 2012 – just one week after her 90th birthday – I got the call saying that Mum had passed.

I was completely beside myself; I couldn't believe that I'd never see her again, that I'd never hear that famous chuckle of hers or kiss her soft cheek.

Demi was also inconsolable. She missed her nan as much as I did and her own mental state started to deteriorate; her anxiety and panic attacks became much worse – so bad, in fact, that she had to leave college halfway through doing her A Levels.

We'd tried to get help for her, of course. She'd been to CAMHS (Child and Adolescent Mental Health Services) before but hadn't really found them very helpful, and after her nan's death, she was referred back to them. She continued attending for counselling until she neared her 18th birthday, and then she was told that if she needed any further treatment, she would have to go to the adult mental health services instead.

Before long, it was the day of the funeral, and although it was obviously a very sad day, it was absolutely packed with friends and family, all of whom truly loved my Mum. Demi was extremely brave, standing in front of them all and reading out her memories of her nan. Some of it wasn't audible as she was crying so much, but I was so proud of her for doing it, as I knew my Mum would be too, looking down at her from Heaven.

To this day, Demi is still struggling, experiencing panic attacks and suffering from depression, which is extremely hard for me to watch. I will carry the guilt of what she's gone through – and is still going through – with me to the end of my days.

She's back in college now, having had to re-sit her first year of her A Levels, and is on anti-depressants to help her through. However, not only does she have to put up with her mental health issues, but she also has a femoral neck anteversion (a twisted thigh bone) which puts her in great pain.

Despite all of this though, she fights the fight every day and never gives up. I couldn't love her any more than I do, and I am the proudest mum walking this earth.

The Doctor Told You What?

Just before my mum died, my brother Al had been diagnosed with bladder cancer and had had his bladder removed – another blow to our family. Since Al's divorce, Mum had looked after him, and so when she became ill and later passed away, I felt like it was my duty to take over.

One day, Al confided in me about his cancer. "I'm scared, Michelle," he said, obviously feeling completely helpless. "What if the big C kills me?"

I tried to comfort him, telling him I'd be with him every step of the way, and agreeing to go with him for his next MRI scan. "Don't think about it," I suggested, knowing that was easier said than done, "they can do all sorts nowadays." He didn't respond to that, just moved closer and hugged me. I didn't know what else to say.

Al and I hadn't always got on, and that's putting it lightly; he had always been extremely short-tempered, forever shouting and creating unnecessary drama, most of which was aimed at Mum. Because of this, I would try and stand up to him, and our arguments sometimes became physical, which distressed my mum even more.

On one occasion, I walked into Mum's house to find her at the bottom of the stairs, and when I asked her what had happened, she told me that Al had pushed past her in a rage, knocking her over and causing her to fall down the stairs. I was so angry that I chased him around the house until he locked himself in the bathroom. Then, I just kept hammering on the door, promising all kinds of revenge for when he eventually came out.

Mum was really upset by now, telling me to leave him alone as I'd just make things worse, and that he didn't mean it.

I responded by telling her how I felt. "I'm fed up of it. He goes on like he owns the place, always shouting and hollering, and I can see that you let him get away with it because you're afraid of him. Well, I'm not scared of him."

Mum told me that she wasn't afraid of him, and when I said she didn't have to put up with him in the house, she just said sadly, "If he's here, I'm not alone."

Eventually, Al came out of the bathroom and apologised, saying that he didn't mean to make her fall, but I still wasn't having it, telling him that she was an old lady now and he had to keep calm and be more careful around her.

He didn't say anything to this, just stared at the floor for a while and then asked Mum if she wanted some tea. That was it – the moment was over, and it wasn't mentioned again.

Once he'd been diagnosed with bladder cancer, he did mellow out a bit; he wasn't as loud or as aggressive anymore, and as I tried to help him get through his illness, we left all of the bad things that had happened between us in the past.

So, I went with Al to his MRI scan, and as we waited for the results, Al spoke of anything and everything apart from the cancer.

That was his way of dealing with it; he thought that if he avoided the subject completely, it would somehow make it less real.

Eventually, the results came back, and the consultant told us that they'd found a tumour in his kidney. At those words, Al's face paled so much I thought he was going to keel over there and then, but instead he just sat in his chair, completely rigid.

As Al wasn't saying anything, I asked the question, "Is it cancerous?" to which the doctor replied that Al would have to come into the hospital to have a biopsy taken. He told Al that they could go in where his colostomy bag was fitted so they wouldn't have to open him up again, and Al just nodded, before going on to talk about his daughter (who lived with his ex-partner). He didn't want to talk about the tumour, and it was as if he didn't even want to acknowledge the possibility that the cancer had spread.

He said nothing on the way home, and once we were back, I asked him if he understood the situation. "Yes," he replied, "but I don't want to talk about it."

Not wanting to push it, I just kissed him on the cheek and told him that we'd go together to get the results, and a week later, we were back, sitting in the consultant's office.

The whole world seemed to stop spinning as the doctor told us, "I'm afraid the tumour is cancerous and aggressive, but there is some good news – we can remove the kidney and you can live quite healthily with just the one."

The room was completely silent as we took in all of this information, and when I asked when he'd have to come in for the operation, the consultant said that they'd send an admittance date in the post and that it would be "sooner rather than later." Al said nothing.

Yet again, the journey home was silent, and though I tried to tell my brother that everything was going to be OK, I wasn't quite sure I even believed it myself.

Around that time, Al lost a lot of weight quite rapidly, and as he was so weak, I arranged for some home care for him. Every Sunday, I would pick him up and take him to Sharon's house for a roast dinner, as well as visiting him during the week to help him with his shopping.

The whole time I prayed for the letter from the hospital, hoping that it would come quickly and that he would be OK.

One Wednesday morning, I went to my own GP for a blood pressure check, taking Coleen's daughter Chelsey with me for the ride. When I walked into the doctor's office, I immediately thought that the atmosphere seemed a little odd… like there was tension in the air but I didn't know why.

Soon, the doctor came and asked the receptionist if she could "take the little one out," and my stomach immediately dropped – what was going on here?

I told the doctor that I'd just come for a blood pressure check, and that there was nothing to worry about, while at the same time knowing there *was* something to worry about; I just didn't know what it was yet.

The GP then took my hand in his and said, "I've got something terrible to tell you." Well, my mind went wild, thinking I must have had some kind of incurable disease or something, but then he continued, "The police called the surgery just now. They'd been trying to contact your family but hadn't been able to get hold of anyone."

I just kept staring at him, wondering what the hell he was talking about.

"It's your brother," he said. "He's dead."

I sat there for quite a while in silence, trying to make sense of what he was telling me. Surely there must be some sort of mistake?

"Michelle," he said again, "did you hear me? I'm afraid your brother Al has passed away."

The way the doctor said his name brought everything back into focus then, but I still couldn't believe what I was hearing. "No, you're wrong," I said. "I picked him up on Sunday for dinner and he was fine. He's having his operation soon, he can't be dead!"

"I'm sorry," the GP replied quietly. "They want you to go and identify his body – he's still at home, they haven't moved him. Again, I'm so sorry, Michelle."

As I stood up, I felt like I was in some kind of dream, and as I walked out of the surgery to collect my little niece, the staff looked at me with concern; they must have known what had happened too.

I sat in the car for a while trying to take in what I'd just been told, and then I phoned my sister Sharon. She must have thought I'd gone mad as I started rambling on, and when she asked me to slow down and explain, I told her that Al was dead. Sharon found this just as difficult to wrap her head around as I had, but after I told her about the doctor and the police trying to contact people, she seemed to get the message.

The line went quiet for a while and then Sharon finally said, "I'll let everyone know." When I told her that I had to go and identify him, I heard Coleen in the background say that she would go with me.

"OK," I whispered, grateful but still not really able to take all this in, "I'm on my way."

When Coleen and I got to Al's flat in Woolwich, we sat for a while in the car, psyching ourselves up. "Ready?" I asked her eventually.

"Ready," she replied.

The lady who worked in the office for the warden-controlled flat let us in, apologising that she hadn't been able to get in touch with me personally. "The police are upstairs with Al now," she continued. "Would you like me to come up with you?"

I told her that no, my niece was with me, and we got into the lift that would take us up to the second floor.

When we stepped out, there were two police officers waiting outside Al's door. "I'm really sorry for your loss," they both said in unison, after I'd introduced myself and Coleen. "Are you ready to go in?" one of them added.

I wasn't really ready at all, but I knew I had to do this, so I followed Coleen in and started walking around the flat.

There was no one in the living area, and as I started walking towards Al's bed (which was just behind a wall), I saw him: his feet were sticking out. I stopped for a while, telling Coleen what I'd seen, and then continued to walk over to him.

There he was: my brother, lying on the floor. His eyes were wide open and an expression of shock was engraved into his face. He still had one arm raised in the air.

Turning to one of the police officers, I stated, "This is my brother." In response, he shuffled his feet and mumbled something about giving us some time alone.

Coleen looked how I felt: she was rooted to the spot, taking in the sight before her, her face pale. She didn't say anything.

Slowly, I moved over to the bed, sitting on it as I took Al's hand. Although his body was cold and rigid, his hand felt supple in mine. "Oh Al," I said, staring at my brother as I stroked his hand. After a while, I said the Lord's Prayer over his body as I thought about the weeks leading up to this point. He'd seemed fine on Sunday – how could this happen in just a few days?

With that, the tears began to flow.

When they came to remove his body, I went back down to the office, not wanting to watch him being zipped up into a black bag, and soon, the lady in the office started talking to me. "He'd been unwell yesterday; he'd been vomiting."

This broke me out of my reverie. "Then why the hell didn't anyone call me yesterday?" I asked through gritted teeth. "I may have been able to do something!"

"I asked him if I should call you, or a doctor," she replied, "but he refused. He said he'd be OK and that he just had an upset stomach. Then, when his home help came in this morning, he was there on the floor."

I was so angry. "You still had a right to call me, especially knowing how ill he'd been."

She just looked at the floor, saying nothing.

Back outside, Coleen and I sat in the car while they brought Al out, placing him in the back of a black van.

"His eyes were still open," whispered Coleen, obviously picturing how Al had looked on the floor. "It freaked me out."

I agreed – it had freaked me out too. I also didn't like that look of shock that was on his face, like he'd been scared and didn't know what was happening to him. It was just so awful.

With that, we made our way back to my sister Sharon's house, where Lydia and Demi were also waiting for us. Lydia told me she'd informed my brother Billy and my sister Pam – both of whom lived in Spain – and that they'd get flights over as soon as they could. I nodded, still feeling extremely numb.

I sat there for a few more hours, going over what the doctor had told me and what we'd seen when we went to Al's flat. The more we talked about it, however, the more surreal it seemed to be.

We were all just in such total shock. No one could believe that this had happened. Why had he died so suddenly? Why had he been taken away from us only a couple of months after Mum had passed away? Why?

Farewell Al

Just nine weeks after my Mum had died, I was arranging the cremation for my brother. I couldn't believe it.

As I was disabled and unable to work, I'd had to get a funeral grant to help towards my Mum's funeral, with the rest gradually being paid off by me and other family members.

Now I was filling in the exact same form for Al, but unfortunately the funeral parlour wouldn't give me another payment plan for the part that the grant didn't cover – it all had to be paid up front.

I was told, therefore, that my brother would have to stay in the morgue until I could come up with the full amount for his cremation, and even after cutting back where we could, there was still a considerable amount left outstanding. My sister Lydia had asked our brother-in-law in Spain to loan us the money to cover the shortfall, but he refused, and I was starting to feel desperate now: I couldn't let my brother lie in the morgue for I don't know how long, I just couldn't do it.

Then I had an idea: during his lifetime, Al had collected coins as a hobby, and he had quite a few silver and gold ones. I decided that we'd have to sell these to help pay off his funeral, but I had no idea where to start. I had a look online to try and find the value of some of the coins, but I needed a buyer and I didn't know how long it would take to get one.

I was at my wit's end when I placed a phone call to my Aunt Margaret (my mum's sister), and I was sobbing as I explained the situation. I'd become very close to Margaret after Mum had passed, and when she said that she would loan me the money to cover the outstanding amount, I cried – I was so relieved.

"Thank you so much!" I said, sobbing. "I don't know what we would have done without you." I told her that as soon as I found a buyer for Al's coins, I would pay her back.

"Well," she replied, "there's no way I would have left him lying in the morgue. We're family."

I could have hugged her right there and then over the phone.

So, I paid for the funeral and the date was arranged. I still felt extremely bad that we had to cut back on a few things – such as having our loved ones round the night before the service – but it would have cost money we simply didn't have.

I took on the job of taking my brother's clothes to the funeral parlour – the same ones he'd worn to our Mum's burial – and asked to see him once he'd been dressed. The room I was led into smelled of disinfectant, and as I walked over to the open coffin, I steeled myself for what I'd see.

He had a lot of make up on, which was probably to hide the discolouration due to the amount of time he'd been there, but he was still my brother. I leant over to kiss his cold cheek, whispered, "Goodbye, Al," and left the room.

When the hearse pulled up outside Sharon's house, I couldn't help but think of all the same people, standing shoulder to shoulder and watching the pall-bearers carry my mum's coffin out of the same door just nine weeks earlier. The pain was still so raw, and my family were being ripped apart by all the losses we'd suffered.

At the church, me, my brother Billy, two of my nephews, and Al's daughter carried my brother's coffin towards the altar to the song, 'He Ain't Heavy He's My Brother'. Afterwards, we sat in our seats, lost in our own thoughts and still stinging from the loss of our mother as we said goodbye to our brother.

A few days later, I went back to collect the ashes, arranging for Aunt Margaret and other family members to meet at Mum's grave so we could scatter them there. After we said the Lord's Prayer, I whispered, "Look after one another."

My heart lay heavy in my chest, as I still blamed myself for the passing of our loved ones. I felt like I was being punished once again by what I'd let that animal do to me as a child.

In the end, I did manage to sell Al's coins to a coin shop in Bromley, so I could pay my aunt back the money I owed her, and I will be forever grateful to her for helping us out. She allowed us to lay our brother to rest.

A while after the funeral, we got the autopsy report back. Al's scar tissue had built up from his previous operations, causing a blockage in his bowel which had then burst suddenly. I cried to think of the pain and shock he must have been in when he died, and I hated the fact that he was all alone when it happened.

In my opinion, the operation that should have saved him actually took his life.

Rest In Peace Al – 29/12/1943 – 14/09/2012.

Deciding To No Longer Be A Victim

My family and I have experienced a lot of grief over the years – far more than any one family should have to go through – and I would like to spend a little time trying to convey how this world has nearly destroyed me.

To say that mental health issues can affect anyone is an understatement; I've seen first-hand how this awful, debilitating condition can swarm through a family like fire through a forest. This illness can take over your life until you simply don't know who you are anymore, let alone your loved ones.

Maybe if I'd spoken out earlier – when I was a child and when my abuse first started – then I could have avoided suffering from this disorder, but it isn't as simple as that. A child's mind is so easy to control and manipulate, and after all, are we not told when we're young to listen to and obey our elders?

I will always feel guilty about the effect my own illness has had on my daughter, with her depression and her panic and anxiety attacks. As mothers, we are supposed to protect our children, to shield them from anything bad or harmful in this world, but my illness did the opposite for Demi.

At the time, I thought I could hide how I was feeling behind my false smile and my fake, happy-go-lucky attitude, but all I did in seeking help so late was allow the mental health of both myself and my family to engulf us in its dark shadow. By the time I realised this, my daughter had already been heavily affected.

I would like to take this opportunity to say that I am sorry, Demi, for everything you witnessed, sorry that I didn't shield you from the negativity surrounding our home, and sorry that you became burdened with the load you still carry today. If I could go back in time and pinpoint the exact moment you went from being a happy child to a lost teenager, I would change it all in an instant.

From the bottom of my heart, I tell you this: I love you and I am incredibly proud of you. You are a strong, intelligent young woman, and I believe you will move onwards and upwards, shaking off the chains of your mental health issues and achieving everything that they're currently holding you back from. You will accomplish amazing things in life, I know you will.

Children have small voices and an overwhelming need both to please and to be loved, and I hope that my story allows our voices to be heard on behalf of the young and vulnerable all around the world. I want my tale to make us aware that many people are abused by someone they know, and to teach our children that it is OK to speak up – that we *will* believe them, no matter what their tormentors may say or who they may be.

I still have nightmares of what I had to suffer while I was so young, but my dreams are bigger than that, much bigger. I have dreams of a world where the unjust get punished, and where the arms of a family is a safe haven for a child and not somewhere they're afraid to be.

Self-harming was the way I found release from my pain, and suicide was the way my niece and nephew found their release. It's strange how we punish ourselves for the wrongs done against us – whether with a cut, an overdose, or death – while a lot of wrongdoers go completely unpunished.

I was one of the lucky ones, as my abuser died, but right now, at this very minute, someone somewhere is being raped, beaten, verbally broken, or all three. Sometimes I look at the drawn curtains in my street and wonder what's going on behind them. We simply cannot be blind to others' suffering, and we can no longer not get involved.

So many people have so many excuses: 'I didn't want to get involved, it's got nothing to do with me, she deserved it – did you see what she was wearing?' That person suffering could be your mum, your sister, or your daughter, and it has to stop.

What type of legal system do we have where jail isn't a deterrent? Where sexual predators go to prison only to come out and immediately reoffend? My belief is that the power they feel – the overwhelming feeling of control – is so strong that even being locked up can't contain it. We can, however, take away that power if we break our silence and start speaking out, now.

My depression, my anxiety and my fear of the outside world are all still controlled by medication, and sometimes I think I'm better and come off them, only to go spiralling once again into the pits of Hell.

My mental health issues are my battle scars, the results of constantly fighting to keep my head above water and to not let the all-consuming dark cloud engulf me, but I feel somewhat lighter after writing 'Why?'. I no longer blame myself for what happened – I see now that I was just a child without a voice, like many other children out there.

Today I am proud to say that I'm a survivor, and believe me, it's a whole lot better than being a victim. I can't go back and undo the past, but what I can do is move forward and watch my daughter grow up into the amazing young woman she is. I refuse to let what happened keep me in that room with that animal, reliving it over and over again in my nightmares.

This book is the key to my prison cell, and I will not be returning.

Just as a bone can be broken, so too can the mind become ill. We have to take our time to heal, to get over the exhausting struggles and to work through our pain at our own pace.

I tried to shoulder the burden of everybody's problems, as well as their worries and grief, and in return I ignored my own. I have learnt that it is OK to be a little selfish, to say no sometimes and to take some time out. We heal at our own pace and in our own time, there's no rush.

Writing 'Why?' has helped me greatly in my healing process, and while I'm not saying that there will never be dark days again, now I take each day as it comes. I realised that I had to tell my story in order to put some ghosts to rest, as well as for the sanity of myself and of others, and I'm pleased that I did.

I may never know the answer to my biggest question, but I know what I'm going to do, and that's continue to heal, continue to grow, and continue to love.

You owned me once, those days are gone,
You thought I would break but I went on,
I have broken the silence, I have spoken out
And now beyond a shadow of a doubt
I am a survivor, a victim no more.

Acknowledgements

I'd like to thank my daughter, Demi. If it weren't for you, I wouldn't be here today. This book is also in remembrance of all those I have loved and lost – you will never be forgotten.

To my baby ♥ Wendy
all my love always
Michelle ♥ ♥ ♥

Printed in Great Britain
by Amazon